I CAN MAKE YOU RICH

www.rbooks.co.uk

Also by Paul McKenna

QUIT SMOKING TODAY

INSTANT CONFIDENCE

I CAN MAKE YOU THIN

I CAN MAKE YOU THIN: 90-DAY SUCCESS JOURNAL

CHANGE YOUR LIFE IN SEVEN DAYS

I CAN MEND YOUR BROKEN HEART (with Hugh Willbourn)

THE HYPNOTIC WORLD OF PAUL McKENNA

I CAN MAKE YOU RICH

PAUL McKENNA Ph.D.

Edited by Michael Neill

BANTAM PRESS

LONDON · TORONTO · SYDNEY · AUCKLAND · JOHANNESBURG

TRANSWORLD PUBLISHERS
61–63 Uxbridge Road, London W5 5SA
A Random House Group Company
www.rbooks.co.uk

First published in Great Britain
in 2007 by Bantam Press
an imprint of Transworld Publishers
This edition published in 2008

Copyright © Paul McKenna 2007, 2008

Paul McKenna has asserted his right under the Copyright, Designs
and Patents Act 1988 to be identified as the author of this work.

A CIP catalogue record for this book
is available from the British Library.

ISBN 9780593060513

Illustrations © Gillian Blease 2007
Text design by Fiona Andreanelli

Addresses for Random House Group Ltd companies outside the UK
can be found at: www.randomhouse.co.uk
The Random House Group Ltd Reg. No. 954009

The Random House Group Ltd makes every effort to ensure that the papers used in
its books are made from trees that have been legally sourced from well-managed and
credibly certified forests. Our paper procurement policy can be found at:
www.randomhouse.co.uk/paper.htm

Printed and bound in Great Britain by
Clays Ltd, Bungay, Suffolk

2 4 6 8 10 9 7 5 3 1

I CAN MAKE YOU RICH

CONTENTS

ACKNOWLEDGEMENTS

I wish to thank all the people who allowed me to ask them endless questions during the writing of this book, especially Sir David Barclay, Sir Richard Branson, Stelios Haji-Ioannou, Sir Philip Green, Peter Jones, Sol Kerzner and Dame Anita Roddick.

I would also like to thank Dr Richard Bandler, Dr Roger Callahan, Dr Ronald Ruden, Dr Robert Holden, Dr Chris Dewberry, Clare Staples, David Stevenson, Michael Breen, Paul Duddridge, Mari Roberts, Doug Young, Larry Finlay, Robert Kirby, Sue Crowley, Kevin Billett and Brandon Bays.

My greatest thanks in writing this book are to Michael Neill, whose dedication and effort has been exceptional. It is a privilege working with you, Michael.

FOREWORD

As someone who started their career in the music industry, I've lost count of the number of songs that feature the word 'money'. It's one theme that appears in new songs around the world every day.

But becoming rich isn't just about piling up the money. Far from it. To be successful these days, you need to be rich in happiness, friendships, health and ideas.

Many new opportunities that are just waiting to be explored emerge from ideas. Today, I dedicate around 40 per cent of my time to new ideas, and spend the rest helping to run and promote the 250 Virgin businesses around the world.

Ideas can emerge any time, anywhere and often when you're least expecting them. It's what you create with these ideas that can make a difference to all of our lives. With that difference, the rewards can follow.

This book taps into these opportunities and offers advice on how to become rich, or get richer. It offers real insights into the worlds of those who've achieved success and is one of the most original books I've ever seen about wealth.

So, get reading and good luck. And remember, if you work hard, you can then play hard.

Sir Richard Branson
Founder, Virgin Group

INTRODUCTION

How to Use This System

HOW TO USE THIS SYSTEM

You are about to become rich!

I don't care what your current financial situation is – what obstacles you might be facing or what challenges you have had to deal with in the past. Wherever you are, however much or little you have, you can change your life and your financial future beginning today.

Every single person I have taught this system to has made more money. Some made a few hundred, some thousands, some millions, each according to their desire and willingness to change old habits and try new things. More importantly, they have each experienced the greater freedom that comes with a rich mindset. Now, it's your turn!

As you will soon find out, this book is very different to just about every other 'money' one you may have seen. It's not filled with prescriptions about how you should invest in the stock market or buy property. It's not a 'money diet' and it's most definitely not about 'get rich quick' schemes.

While you will undoubtedly make more money as a result of reading this book, doing the exercises and listening to the hypnosis CD, you will get so much more. You will experience a way of living happily in the world no matter how much money you have. And let's face it – if you're having fun and living well, you can afford to take your time and do things right.

Indeed, the fact that you're reading this now shows that you have already made one of the most important investments in your life – the investment in yourself, your mindsets and your skills.

This book is divided into two distinct sections. Part one, 'The Psychology of Wealth', will introduce you to the core principles, beliefs and attitudes that enable certain people to thrive regardless of their current circumstances. You will learn how to think rich, transform your relationship with money, master fear and greed, and turn up the temperature on something I call your 'wealth thermostat'.

In addition, you will learn to overcome emotional spending. For many people, this is one of the most important chapters in this book, and I have seen people save thousands of pounds and propel themselves out of debt simply by applying the principles in this chapter. We will finish this section of the book by setting a clear direction for where you want to go in your life – a compelling vision of a rich and happy future.

Part two of the book is packed with everything you need to know to actively go out and make more money in the world. Whether you are just starting out or are already a seasoned traveller on the road to wealth, each of the chapters and every exercise will help program your mind to automatically seek out the best available wisdom on how, when and where to create and use your money.

In our final chapter together, I will share some of the secrets of living rich, regardless of how much money you may currently have in the bank. As you work with these ideas, you will experience more and more of what you really want – an ongoing sense of happiness and freedom that is priceless!

Just by reading, doing the exercises and listening to the hypnosis CD, you will find your investment of time and money in this book will be repaid thousands of times over. Simply follow my instructions and your life will begin to change for the better.

In fact, you won't be able to stop yourself – once your mind is positively directed towards wealth, it begins to create a domino effect, creating positive changes in your life and the lives of the people around you that could never have been predicted when you began.

A quick word about the CD

While the mind-programming exercises on the CD will have a powerful impact in and of themselves, they are designed to activate certain suggestions and strategies I have installed throughout the book. For maximum effect, I recommend you use the CD in conjunction with the book.

Where did the ideas in this book come from?

This book is not based on some abstract theories, but upon a new understanding of how to get the most out of the amazing wealth-creating potential of your mind. In assembling this system, I have spent time personally with some of the world's richest men and women and asked them questions that would reveal their innermost beliefs and strategies for success.

> *The real source of wealth and capital in this new era is not material things. It is the human mind, the human spirit, the human imagination, and our faith in the future.*
>
> STEVE FORBES, billionaire publisher

This is not a biography of these people – it is a specific, applicable model of how YOU can become rich by teaching yourself to think and act in similar ways to some of the most successful people in our society.

Just as a master chef brings a dash of inspiration to any recipe, any master of excellence first follows a specific sequence of thoughts and behaviours that allows them to consistently achieve phenomenal results. That dash of inspiration that makes their success unique to them is the one ingredient you will have to provide to bring the ideas in this book to life – everything else you need to succeed is provided for you.

As you read this book it will become easier to understand. Making money is like any other skillset. You don't need to stop being yourself in order to learn it – you just need to open your mind to thinking about your life in brand new ways.

This book and the accompanying CD comprise a system that will help you to install a 'rich mindset' in yourself. This has been shown to cause people to think more positively, creatively and optimistically about making money and having a richer life.

What I will give you here is the mindset of some of the wealthiest people in our culture, and an invitation to join them by taking advantage of the two things they have that you have too – a creative mind and a 24-hour day. The difference between them and you is not in what you have – it is in how you choose to use it.

Over the years, I have watched my own wealth grow in direct connection to my willingness to apply what I was learning. Yet when I first set out to create more money in my life, I wondered whether it was even possible. I found it difficult to 'see myself rich', and even more difficult to imagine how quickly and easily it could happen.

Unlike so many of the people selling wealth courses I am not going to be suggesting that you emulate me, or even that you emulate the many wonderful people who contributed to the effectiveness of the system you are about to learn. Instead, I want you to become the richest, happiest, most successful version of yourself.

I now know for a fact that it is possible not only to create wealth, but to change the quality of your life for the better as you do it. The small investment in time you make to read this book and listen to the hypnosis CD will be paid back many times over.

I've designed this system to make it as easy as possible for you to change your life and the lives of the people around you for the better. Because, as you will soon realize, being rich isn't just about you – it's about how you impact the world around you and the legacy you leave behind.

One final thought

As you read this book you will have moments of insight when suddenly you will become conscious of your beliefs and patterns. You will notice which ones support you and which ones you want to change.

Expect some of the ideas in this book to challenge your thinking!

As you read this book and go through each of the exercises in turn, it will become easier and easier to understand. Just becoming aware of your current thoughts will begin the process of change, but it's the techniques we will begin doing shortly that will quickly reprogram your unconscious mind and positively alter your financial blueprint. Your life will become richer, and you will experience more happiness and greater freedom than ever before.

Making money is just a skill, but becoming rich is an art. This book is about both the skill of making money and the art of becoming rich. So if all that happened as a result of your working with this system was that you made more money, our work would only be half done. You need to be happier in yourself and feel truly richer in your life!

The world doesn't need more miserable millionaires – it needs people who are living their lives with freedom, artistry and joy. When you get richer, the world becomes a better place. So as you read this book we are going to take you beyond your limitations as you become the most amazing possibility of you!

To your success,

Paul McKenna

PART ONE

The Psychology of Wealth

CHAPTER ONE

Getting Rich Is an Inside Job

GETTING RICH IS AN INSIDE JOB

What do you think of when you think of being rich?

Do you imagine fancy cars, large homes and world travel?

Do you think about fat men in expensive suits, smoking big cigars and looking around the room to see whose is the biggest?

Do you imagine being able to make large donations to your favourite charities and creating a genuine and tangible difference in the world?

Each one of these 'daydreams' reveals your current thinking, which is either holding you back or propelling you forward towards experiencing greater riches in your life.

When you are truly rich you will not only have more than enough money, you will know that you can always create still more. Therefore, you will never fear not having enough and you will feel an inner confidence and happiness.

So when I talk about 'being rich' throughout this book, I will be talking about one thing:

**Being rich is living your life on your own terms –
according to your possibilities, not your limitations.**

What you may not yet realize is that you are already richer than you think.

Let me ask you this – if you had all the money in the world, how much of your life would you actually change?

Would you change your friends?

Would you change your job?

Would you change what you laugh at?

Would you change where you live?

Would you change what you drive?

Would you change what you eat?

Would you change what you wear?

Every question that you answered 'no' to is an area in your life where you are already living rich. Any question you answered 'yes' to is an area where you'd be richer – and that's what the system in this book will help you achieve.

But if you're not rich yet, it's not your fault, it's not your parents' fault, and it's not even society or the government or fate that's to blame. It's just an indication that your current wealth programming isn't as good as it can be. Your mind is like a computer – and, like a computer, it's only as effective as the software it's running.

The power of a single thought

Almost eighty years ago, one of the richest men in the world was the legendary industrialist Andrew Carnegie. He was convinced that he had discovered the real secret of creating wealth, and commissioned a young reporter named Napoleon Hill to interview 400 of the richest people alive to see if they too had used this secret to create their fortunes.

Hill spent the next twenty years meeting up with nearly every person on the list, and discovered that, without fail, they had followed the same simple blueprint for wealth. The book he eventually published, *Think and Grow Rich*, has become one of the bestselling non-fiction books of all time.

The secret Carnegie and all the great achievers used to create riches in their lives was simply this:

All wealth is created with the human mind.

Look around you – how many things can you see right where you are sitting that began as a thought in someone's mind?

Are you sitting on a piece of furniture? Are you inside a building or a train or on a bench? Even if you are sitting in a park, that park began as a thought in someone's mind.

Do you drive a car, or travel by bus? At one time, oil was not considered to be of any use – it was essentially a waste product. Someone's mind turned it from a waste product into one of the most valuable commodities in the world today.

What will be the next big idea? More to the point, who will have it?

Even more to the point, why not you?

I often hear people say that the rich are just lucky, or that they work harder, or they are dishonest, but the truth is much simpler:

The difference between the rich and the poor is that the rich have learned to recognize the value of their thoughts.

Rich thinker, Poor thinker

> *Wealth is the product of man's ability to think.*
>
> AYN RAND,
> novelist and philosopher

One of the most important things I learned early on in my study of wealth is that you can't necessarily spot the richness of a person's life by the car they drive or the size of their bank account. That is why I will not be referring to 'rich people' or 'poor people' in this book – as far as I am concerned, there's no such thing. What there is, is a tremendous difference between people who 'think rich' and those who 'think poor'.

'Rich thinkers' will be rich regardless of the current size of their bank balance – they will always be looking for possibilities and living life on their terms. If they are temporarily low on cash, they won't be for long, and they somehow always seem to find a way to do what they really want to do in their lives.

'Poor thinkers', on the other hand, may have big houses and wear fancy clothes, but their heads are filled with fears about the future and mistrust of those around them. Because they don't know that they would be all right even if all their money disappeared, they are forced to continually try to protect what they have or grab more from others.

Rich thinkers are not necessarily the best educated or most naturally gifted people you will meet, though some of them are – they simply think differently about money than most of society. They realize that making money is neither a mysterious process nor a cosmic reward – it is just a skill, like learning to juggle or riding a bike.

Once you have mastered that skill, you will be able to make money wherever you are and whatever is going on in the world around you. Until you have mastered the skill, you may find yourself struggling even while people prosper all around you.

That's why you could take away all of Richard Branson's or Anita Roddick's money and in a very short space of time they would have it all back – simply because the one thing you cannot take away from them is their ability to think rich and make money as a result.

This is the first key to your success – recognizing that your riches are not in some far-off place, but that they are waiting for you to find them inside your mind, right where you are sitting now. And if you're going to go inside your mind to find them, it's useful to begin with a clear understanding of the territory you're about to explore.

How your mind *really* works

I remember as a child going on a camping trip with my family. On the first night, the evening sky was dark and clouds obscured what little light the moon was shedding on things. Because I was unfamiliar with the area, I was frightened.

Fortunately, I had a torch. At first I only shone the torch in the direction of the next scary noise, and consequently I got no real sense of the territory that surrounded me. But after a time, I became curious as to what the landscape looked like. The next day, I spent time exploring the lie of the land with my parents.

By the second night, even though I was still limited to a torch, I was no longer scared by what I could not yet see. I knew the territory well enough to know that as long as I took my time and paid attention to what I was doing, I would be safe.

Now let's put it into the context of making money. If you are not yet familiar with the world of money, it may seem strange and even a little bit frightening. You might be reluctant to try certain things because you're not quite sure where they will take you. But if you are willing to let me be your guide, I will introduce you to both the basics of money and your own internal 'torch' – the amazing world of your mind.

While I have explained some of this in my previous books, in order to succeed it is absolutely essential to understand the real differences between your conscious and unconscious minds.

Your conscious mind

There are only two primary ways we make sense of the world – consciously and unconsciously. Throughout this book, I will be referring to them as your conscious and unconscious mind.

Your conscious mind is the mind that you actively and deliberately think with all day long. You probably experience it as a fairly continual internal voice that you think of as 'me'.

But while the conscious mind certainly has its uses, it is extremely limited in what it can accomplish on its own. Studies have shown that it can only hold a handful of ideas at any one time. That's why the majority of your life is run automatically by your other mind.

Your unconscious mind

The unconscious mind is your larger mind. It can process millions of messages of sensory information every single second, and contains all of your wisdom, memories and intelligence. It is the source of your creativity, and perhaps most importantly for our purposes here, it stores and runs all the 'programs' of automatic behaviour that you use to live your life.

So the unconscious mind is like having an 'autopilot' function in the brain which allows us to do multiple things simultaneously without having to concentrate on all of them at once. These programs ('habits') are useful because they free our conscious minds up to think about other things. Learning to drive a car involves learning lots of little habits – indicating, accelerating, breaking, turning, etc. After you have practised them consciously several times they become habitual so that now you can just get in the car and decide where you want to go.

But as we shall see, sometimes we need to upgrade our old, outdated programs if we want to change and upgrade our lives. Until your unconscious mind is programmed for wealth, nothing you learn, know or do will make any difference in the long run. You cannot overcome your unconscious programming with logical arguments or even hard work. It is only through the creative application of your imagination that you will reprogram your mind for wealth.

Which direction are you headed in?

Over the last twenty years I have had access to many high achievers and I have been amazed at how some are able to truly enjoy their wealth while others remain trapped by their own limited thinking.

> *Money gives you the freedom to do with your time what you want to do with it.*
>
> RICHARD BRANSON, billionaire

Here are a few examples of how poverty programming can affect even some of the most famous and financially richest people in the world:

- At the time of my writing this, Mariah Carey is worth over $100 million – yet in a recent interview she said that sometimes she still feels financially insecure.

- In a recent interview, the billionaire Martha Stewart said: 'I have a beautiful weekend house in the Hamptons, but it is not, as it turns out, my summer dream house. It doesn't have the view of the ocean that I absolutely want. It doesn't have the rustic wood floors that I absolutely crave. It doesn't have a little dock to which I can tie my little rowboat and it doesn't have the shallow water of a quiet lagoon where I can pick my plants.'

- When asked to confirm the speculation that he was worth over a billion dollars, J. Paul Getty replied: 'Yes, I suppose it's true, but a billion dollars doesn't go as far as it used to.'

- When an elderly John D. Rockefeller learned that members of his family intended to give him a wheelchair to help him get round his estate, he told them: 'If you don't mind, I'd rather have the money.'

I hope by now you are beginning to realize that having a lot of money will never be enough to make you rich. It is the quality of your thoughts that will ultimately create the quality of your life.

As you go through this book and take part in the exercises, you will become more aware of your current tendencies towards both rich thinking and poor thinking.

You will also begin to notice rich thinking and poor thinking in the people around you, and it will become apparent to you how each person's thoughts are taking them in a direction. Rich thinking takes you in the direction of more freedom and greater wealth; poor, impoverished thinking, sometimes described as a 'poverty mentality', focuses you on what you can't have and drives you away from possibility.

You have an infinitely creative mind and an infinite capacity for wealth. You just need to learn how to use it. This system, and in particular the hypnosis CD, will prepare your unconscious mind for riches. Together, we will reprogram your mind to think rich, and in so doing notice the opportunities for wealth that surround you at any moment.

Here is a simple exercise you can do to begin the process right now …

A RICHER LIFE

1. Think about what it would be like to be truly rich – to live your life on your terms, according to your possibilities not your limitations.

   Take a few moments to consider how your life would be better in each of the following areas:

   • Relationships
   • Career
   • Family
   • Health
   • Recreation
   • Spirituality

2. When you have a sense of what some of the positive differences of living a rich life would be, write down the four most important things you would be able to do, be or have as a result:

   a.

   b.

   c.

   d.

   These four things are symbols of the highest values you currently hold around having greater riches in your life. We will refer back to them later in this chapter.

The power of focus

One of the fundamental operating principles we will return to again and again throughout this book is this:

You get more of what you focus on.

If you focus on poverty and lack, you will tend to get more of that in your life. If you focus on the wealth that you already have, you will tend to get more of that as well.

It's vitally important to reprogram your unconscious mind so that you are continually focused on what you want to create – in this case, greater freedom and greater financial abundance. This book and the accompanying CD will train you to do exactly that.

As you begin to feel rich and see yourself as a wealthy person, you will watch your financial abundance grow. As you become richer in your thoughts and emotions, you will experience more and more freedom in your life.

This is not about 'faking it'. Because people often define being rich as no more than having a lot of money, they think the way to feel rich is to act like their idea of 'a millionaire'. They buy expensive clothing and flash cars and jewellery in an attempt to make themselves 'feel' rich.

This can work up to a point, but it often backfires sooner than you would imagine. You may feel rich pulling up to Royal Ascot in your borrowed tuxedo and rented Rolls Royce, but just how rich will you feel when the credit card bill arrives and you have no idea how you'll pay it?

While you will almost certainly begin experiencing money arriving from 'out of the blue' throughout our time together, it is by cultivating the *internal experience* of being rich that your rich life truly begins.

There are essentially two ways to do this. The first is by spotting what I call 'rich moments'.

Stop for a moment and think about something in your life that brings you a sense of pleasure, satisfaction and meaning.

Did you think about someone you love? An activity you enjoy? A beautiful sunset? Your health? Your happiness?

Most people are surprised that those things that bring the greatest sense of richness to their lives only rarely cost a lot of money. Over the next few weeks, you can easily reset your perceptual filters to notice how rich you already are – how much of your life you are already living on your own terms, according to your possibilities, not your limitations.

Here are some of the rich moments I've had today that had nothing to do with money:

- Listening to a CD I love which brings back happy memories.

- Spending time with my friends, just having fun.

- Taking a walk in the park with my dog.

> *If you want to feel rich, just count the things you have that money can't buy.*
>
> OLD PROVERB

We all have moments like this every single day – it's just that we are conditioned to ignore them and focus instead on all the things that we don't like and that are not yet the way we want them to be.

Make it your mission to find lots of areas of your life where you feel rich every day. Start by looking for anything that makes you more aware of the abundance and riches in your daily life. In those moments when you get pleasure from your work, buy something you like, give a donation to a favourite cause, or even walk into a restaurant knowing you can afford to order anything you want, you are having the exact same internal experience as the wealthiest billionaire.

Remember, you get more of what you focus on. The more you practise noticing rich moments throughout your day, the more rich moments you will experience.

The second way to create riches from the inside out is to create your very own associational link to what it feels like to be living your highest values. When you are in connection with your highest values, you will think your richest thoughts and naturally be guided to take the actions that lead to outer riches.

Now try the exercise overleaf. Go through this process at least three times a day *every single day for the next three weeks.* This will reprogram your unconscious mind for wealth in ways that you can only begin to imagine ...

CREATE YOUR RICH ANCHOR

1. Take your list of four things that having money and being rich will give you and write a few words about each one in the numbered boxes.

2. Create a code word that summarizes each phrase and write each code word within the numbered boxes.

3. Vividly imagine exactly what it would be like to achieve the first two goals and as you do so, squeeze your thumb and the middle finger on your right hand together.

4. Ask yourself: Having achieved these two things, what does it do for me, get for me or give me? Write a code word that describes it in the next box along.

5. Vividly imagine exactly what it would be like to achieve the next two goals and as you do squeeze your thumb and the middle finger on your left hand together. Write a code word that describes it in the next box along.

6. Take the answers from steps 4 & 5, pair them together, at the same time squeeze both your thumbs and fingers together on your left & right hands and ask yourself again: Having achieved these two things, what does it do for me, get for me or give me? Write a code word for that in the central box.

7. Squeeze both your thumbs and fingers together on your left & right hands and imagine taking that wealthy feeling into every area of your life. Think to yourself: 'I am rich!'

8. Imagine waking up with that feeling every morning, and see what you will see, hear what you will hear and feel how good it will be feeling this wealthy in your daily life. Make it feel as real as though it's happening right now.

1. _____
_____
_____
_____

[ ]

2. _____
_____
_____
_____

[ ]

[ ]

[ ]

[ ]

[ ]

3. _____
_____
_____
_____

4. _____
_____
_____
_____

FREQUENTLY ASKED QUESTIONS ABOUT 'GETTING RICH IS AN INSIDE JOB'

Q. Is this for real? How do I know you're not just conning me out of £10.99?

Talk about poor thinking! I'm not asking you to put away the discerning part of your mind – far from it. In fact, your ability to assess the difference between someone who wants to contribute to your wealth and someone who wants to separate you from it is one of the most valuable skills of the truly rich.

But if you allow your poor thinking and poverty programming to stop you from even stepping up to the crease, you will never even take the first step on the road to wealth.

Think about it this way – it's not money that will make you a good or bad person. Like power, money is just an amplifier. It doesn't actually corrupt anyone – it reveals who they are on the inside. If you've made the decision to live life on your own terms by living your values, having more money will simply allow you to live those values on a larger scale and have an ever greater positive impact on the world.

Q. But aren't rich people just luckier than everyone else?

First off, there are no 'rich people' or 'poor people' – rich thinking leads to a rich life, no matter how much money you have in the bank. And as for the question of luck, the scientific research shows that's not so. A recent American university study into the effects of what is called 'proactive personality' revealed that those individuals who identify opportunities and act upon them make more money, get promoted more often and are happier in their work.

In other words, we create our own luck by the way we think, feel and act in the world. As champion baseball player and World Series winner Earl Wilson once said, 'Of course success is a matter of luck – just ask any failure!'

Q. How soon will the money start coming in? I've got bills to pay!

As you will see in chapter five, the 'get rich quick' mentality is nearly always driven by the two great enemies of wealth: fear and greed. Making money can take a bit of time, but as you begin to cultivate the energy of wealth and the experience of being rich from the inside out, you will find your life begins to change for the better almost immediately.

CHAPTER TWO

Transforming Your Relationship with Money

TRANSFORMING YOUR RELATIONSHIP WITH MONEY

> *Money doesn't make you happy. Last year I earned $40 million dollars; this year I earned $50 million. I'm not any happier.*
>
> ARNOLD SCHWARZENEGGER, actor and politician

Money is one of the most emotional subjects on the planet. In fact, many people feel more comfortable sharing the intimate details of their sex lives with friends than sharing the intimate details of their finances.

Yet the purpose of money is simply to allow the smooth exchange of goods and services.

So what is it that gives money its emotional power? One answer is that we do. And one way we do it is by giving those pieces of metal or paper, or even numbers on a piece of paper, MEANING.

Sometimes we do this literally, as in 'This paycheque = my phone bill' or 'This £5 note = lunch', so if we lose the £5 note, in our minds, we've just lost our lunch.

Often, the meaning is even more metaphoric. 'Money is freedom of choice' or 'Money is love made visible' or even 'Money is the root of all evil'.

Here's why this is so important:

Whatever meaning you are attaching to money is either drawing it closer or pushing it away.

Trying to live a rich life when you have a poor relationship with money is like trying to drive a car with one foot on the accelerator and the other one on the brakes. You may occasionally make some progress, but in the end no matter how hard you try you never seem to really get anywhere.

So in order to begin letting go of all the things you've been attributing to money that make it more difficult to have, we'll take a closer look at where all these ideas came from in the first place.

Let's begin a few thousand years ago when conch shells were exchanged in a primitive form of barter. People literally 'shelled out' in exchange for food or labour. Then, in the mines of Mesopotamia, workers were paid in salt, or 'salarium', which they could then exchange for goods and services. This is the origin of the idea of working for a 'salary'.

But as trade became more and more complex, the use of commodities like shells and salt was replaced by the use of precious metals. And once trade became more centralized, the direct exchange of precious metals was replaced by the use of IOUs.

Coins were the first officially sanctioned IOUs, followed fairly quickly by pieces of paper that could be exchanged for precious metal. In fact, the pound got its name because until a few hundred years ago, it could be exchanged for a pound-weight of sterling silver. In the late 19th century, an international system was set up called 'the gold standard' which allowed for a universal and stable unit of valuation.

Finally, in the 1940s, the governments of the world decided to abandon the gold standard system. Promises of exchange were replaced by articles of faith – the marketplace's faith that the government that printed it will continue to back it, with or without reserves of gold. In this sense, money no longer has any inherent or intrinsic value. The value of money, whether in the form of euro, yen, dollar or pound, is now based entirely on the value we and others place upon it.

So what is money really?

Whatever we make it up to be.

THE MEANING OF MONEY

1. Complete these twelve sentences about money, wealth and riches to uncover the key elements of your current unconscious programming.

   1. People with money are _____

   2. Money makes people _____

   3. I'd have more money if _____

   4. My parents always thought money would _____

   5. Money causes _____

   6. I'm afraid that if I had more money I would _____

   7. Money is _____

   8. In order to have more money, I would need to _____

   9. I think money _____

  10. If I were really rich, I would _____

  11. My biggest fear about money is _____

  12. Money is _____

2. Circle any of your unconscious beliefs about money that might be holding you back, even if they seem unquestionably 'true' to you.

3. Repeat this exercise daily for at least the next week. You may find some of the deeper programs take a bit longer to come up to the surface.

What did you discover? Are your beliefs and associations with money those of someone who is programmed for poverty or for riches?

By heightening our awareness of our beliefs about money, we can begin to make sense of many of our emotions and behaviours when dealing with it, and by changing them, we can transform the emotional impact of money in our lives. After all, would you rather work half your life for freedom of choice or for the root of all evil?

Here are some of the most common beliefs people hold that keep them from creating an abundance of money in their lives:

• **Money corrupts.**
There is an inherent mistrust of wealth in our society, most of it based on the underlying assumption that money corrupts. But the reality is, money doesn't corrupt – it reveals. Many wonderful people are doing amazingly positive things with their money. Why not you?

• **There is not enough money to go round.**
Money is not a zero-sum game – it's an infinite game, and the more people who are playing it the more money there is to go around. Provided you are spending money and not just hoarding it, the more money you make the more money will be circulating in the system. In this sense, the richer you become, the richer you will be making others.

- **I don't want to make money because I'm scared that I will lose it.**

That makes about as much sense as saying I don't want to eat a nice meal because I'm scared that I'll have to flush it down the toilet later. The purpose of money isn't to keep it for ever, it's to use it. And once you learn the secrets of making money, which I will share with you in the second part of this book, you'll realize that as long as you have the capacity to think, you have the ability to make more money.

In order to question some of your own limiting beliefs about money, do this simple exercise adapted from Patricia Remele's book, *Money Freedom*. It's based on the idea that when you take away all of our culturally imposed beliefs about what it should and shouldn't be, money is simply a tool we can use to make our lives easier and reach our goals faster. Therefore what is true about money must be true about other tools as well …

THE SHOVEL EXERCISE

1. Make a list of the most negative-seeming beliefs about money you uncovered in the previous exercise.

2. Substitute the word 'shovel' (another practical tool) for 'money' in each of the sentences on your list. Notice whether the statements still make sense or have any emotional significance.

   Examples:

   'The love of shovels is the root of all evil.'

   'Shovels don't grow on trees.'

   'I feel guilty because I have more shovels than my father ever did.'

   Remember, the idea here is to simply take away the emotional 'sting' from these ideas – it doesn't matter whether or not you really believe them.

Where do all these ideas about money come from?

When we are born, our mind is a clean slate. There are certain things our bodies are genetically programmed to be able to do almost from birth – the basics of movement, communication and self-healing. However, when it comes to what we choose to believe about the world, our minds are up for grabs.

Before the age of seven a child doesn't know enough to be able to rely on their own judgement and reasoning. Their critical faculties are undeveloped. A critical faculty is the ability to question, judge, analyse, criticize and, very importantly, compare.

It is because children haven't developed this critical faculty that they can believe in Father Christmas and fairies as easily as they believe in geometry and money.

> *Lack of money is the root of all evil.*
>
> GEORGE BERNARD SHAW,
> Nobel Prize-winning writer

Until we take control of our own minds, our beliefs about the world and ourselves come from the continual messages that we receive in the first few years of our lives. What we are told again and again, particularly at moments of emotional intensity, has the most powerful effect upon us. In fact, anything that is said at a moment of emotional intensity has the power of a hypnotic suggestion.

If you believe you have to work hard to make money, you will only sort for jobs that involve a lot of effort. If you believe that everyone is out to rip you off, you will unconsciously find people who will do that. If you believe that you deserve great wealth, then your mind will sort for opportunities that create that.

This is one of the reasons why hypnosis is such a powerful tool for changing your life. It allows you to get right to the part of your brain where the old programs are stored, and literally reprogram your mind for riches.

It's also why the changes you will be able to make as you work through the exercises in this book and listen to the hypnosis CD are likely to be so positive.

Ending financial self-sabotage

Most of us have inherited a mixed bag of positive and some negative beliefs about what having more money in our lives would mean. These beliefs in turn affect how much money we will allow ourselves to have.

For example, how do you react when you read these statements?

- I deserve money.
- Money can come to me easily.
- There's more than enough to go round.
- It's OK for me to be rich.

If they feel comfortable to you as you read them – as obvious and true as saying 'the sky is blue' – chances are you are already living a fairly rich life. If they feel uncomfortable, untrue or even unforgivable, you've just uncovered one of the real blocks to a lifetime of wealth and freedom.

In contrast to the above statements, what were you told as a child about money?

Many of my clients answer with things like this:

- You'll never amount to anything.
- Shame on you – why can't you get anything right?
- It's a good thing you're beautiful, because you aren't smart enough to make it on your own.

There is a long list of beliefs and stories people use to keep themselves away from wealth. Maybe you've thought that if you became rich you'd change as a person, or you'd become a target, or you would lose your friends. Perhaps you've been telling yourself that you won't be able to handle the pressure, or that you don't really care that much about money anyway.

Many people have been taught things like: 'The Bible says money is the root of all evil.' What the Bible actually says is: 'The *love* of money [or, according to some scholars, *'lust for money'*] is the root of all evil' – that is, the pursuit of money for its own sake, as a commodity to be hoarded.

Here's the key:

Whatever negative story about wealth you have told yourself in the past, it's time to let it go.

There's a saying in the world of computer programming:

Garbage in = Garbage out

Your mind is like a computer, but it's only as useful as the programs it's running. And those programs are made up of your most frequent thoughts and most tightly held beliefs. This is why it is so important to let go

> *I have never been in a situation where having money made it worse.*
>
> CLINTON JONES,
> American footballer

of any unconscious ideas you may still be carrying from your childhood about why money is bad or that you're not good enough to have it.

The unconscious mind is not logical. It doesn't stop and think about what you want or what's best for you. It just does whatever it's been programmed to do. In fact, your mind will not allow you to deviate from the programs you hold in your unconscious. It will do whatever it takes to prove these unconscious programs about money to be true.

Over the years I have worked with many clients who have what they refer to as a 'self-sabotage' mechanism. Whenever things are going well for them, it seems as though they manage to screw it up. This is *always* caused by beliefs in the unconscious mind that will not allow them to succeed. All I do is have them reprogram the limiting beliefs and suddenly their life dramatically changes for the better.

For example, I have a friend who was good at creating money, but somehow would always sabotage his efforts to create lasting wealth by finding ways to get rid of his money almost as quickly as he made it. His behaviour around money didn't seem to make any sense until one day he told me of a childhood experience where he had said to his mother that when he grew up, he wanted to be rich. His mother had replied, 'Why do you want to do that? Rich people get heart attacks!'

No wonder he couldn't hang on to his money – in his unconscious mind, having a lot of money equalled death! Remember, the unconscious mind is not logical, it's purposeful – and its number-one purpose is survival. Although he hadn't been conscious of it until that moment, this unsupportive and false belief had been installed at an impressionable age. As soon as he made any money, his unconscious mind worked at getting rid of it 'to keep him alive'.

After just twenty minutes of reprogramming, his unconscious fear of getting a heart attack from having too much money had gone. Within a few months his business went into overdrive, and just over a year later he had created a brand new career for himself and was living the life of his dreams.

Just becoming conscious of your old programs around money is often enough to take away their power. In addition, I will work with your unconscious mind on the CD accompanying this book to reprogram your beliefs and change your thinking and behaviour around money for good.

Undoing cultural hypnosis

One of the tabloid newspapers recently ran a series of articles entitled 'So Rich You Want to Slap Them'. This certainly mirrors the views of a proportion of the population, who are angry with the people who have mastered the art of creating money.

We are continually told that 'there is only a finite amount of wealth' and that 'the more we have, the less there will be for others'. It's common in our culture to hear terms such as 'filthy rich' or 'fat cat', which are indicative of an underlying mistrust of people with money.

This sort of cultural hypnosis creates one of the largest blocks people have about making money and living rich – who they think they'll have to become and what they think they'll have to give up in order to get it.

Some people believe they will have to sacrifice their time, or their health, or even their family to the cause of 'making money at all costs'. Yet when we broaden our definition of rich from 'having a lot of money' to 'living life on our own terms', those sacrifices can all be seen to be unrealistic.

If you had no time, you wouldn't be rich no matter how much money you had. If you don't have your health, you don't have anything – all the money in the world can't buy you another minute of life. And if you give up the love of your family for a few dollars more, your life will only become poorer.

There is, however, one sacrifice you *will* need to make

– you will need to give up your resentment of people who have more money than you!

When I began on my own journey to wealth, I believed (among other things) that:

- The rich get richer and the poor get poorer.
- If I win, others must lose.
- In order for someone to make a lot of money, they have to screw other people over.

You may be holding some similar beliefs for yourself, but here's the simple truth:

If you dislike people with money, it will be difficult to become one of them.

Once I became aware of how much I resented people with money, I became aware of how much that resentment was holding me back in my own pursuit of wealth. I knew I had to change the pattern – to reprogram my automatic, unconscious reaction to people who have money. Even if I didn't like what I thought they had done to get their money, I realized that the only person I was hurting with my resentment was myself. As the saying goes, hanging on to resentment is like drinking poison and expecting the other person to die!

At first, I used a simple system of substitution. Any time I noticed myself grumbling inside my head at the success or wealth of someone else, I would immediately replace that thought with a positive one wishing that person well. It felt strange at first, but each time I did it I noticed I felt a little bit better inside myself.

Then, I learned a technique that enabled me to make even more dramatic changes more quickly. Instead of focusing on what I didn't want (i.e. 'to be like them'), it focused my mind on what I did want – to make money and live rich in an ethical and enjoyable way. Here is what I learned, exactly the way that I practise it to this day …

FROM RESENTMENT TO RICHES

Be sure to read through all the instructions before you begin ...

1. Think about someone whose success or wealth you have been resenting. Create an image in your mind of what they look like. What colour is their hair? What clothes are they wearing? What expression do they have on their face?

2. Now, think about yourself being exactly the way you most want to be – living life on your own terms with the financial assets to do what you really want to be doing. How do you stand, smile and speak? How happy and confident do you look?

3. Shrink down that picture of your rich self so that it fits in one small corner of the picture of the person you have been resenting.

4. Now, switch the pictures as fast as you can! As the picture of the person you have been resenting shrinks down into the corner, expand the picture of your rich self until it fills the screen. Make sure the expanded picture of your rich self is big, bright and bold!

5. Take a moment to clear your mind, then repeat the process at least five times. Make the switch faster and faster each time you do it.

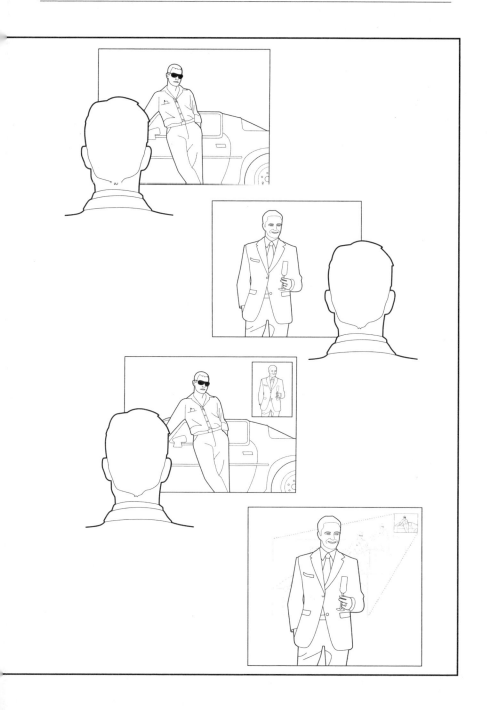

Several years ago, there was a study conducted into happiness and comparative wealth, which was quite revealing. Participants were asked to choose between two scenarios. In the first, they were to be paid $90,000 and their friends and colleagues would all be paid $80,000; in the second, they would receive $100,000 but their friends and colleagues would receive $110,000.

What do you suppose people chose?

If you guessed that they opted for more money, you'd be wrong – an overwhelming majority said they would prefer to have less money as long as it was more than everyone else!

This is poor thinking in its most insidious form – using money as a measure of personal value, status or worth. In contrast, rich thinkers don't use their money to make themselves feel better – they use it to make themselves a richer life.

The more comfortable you become around every person's capacity to make a contribution and create wealth, the easier it becomes for you to do the same. This is one of the absolute keys to rich thinking:

The more comfortable you become with the wealth of others, the faster your own wealth will grow.

Here's one last exercise you can do that will make it easier for you to release any residual negativity around money and become instantly richer in your thinking and actions …

CREATING A RICHER WORLD

1. Think about someone you believe is struggling financially and imagine them wealthy and successful.

2. Think about someone you believe is already doing well and imagine them becoming even more wealthy and successful.

3. Repeat steps 1 & 2 with as many different people as you like until you feel 'clean' – no pity and no resentment.

4. Imagine what the world would be like if there was no poverty and everyone had more than enough to live life on their own terms. How do you feel about living in that world? How do you feel about yourself?

The more often you repeat this exercise, the faster your wealth will grow.

FREQUENTLY ASKED QUESTIONS ABOUT 'TRANSFORMING YOUR RELATIONSHIP WITH MONEY'

Q. It's all well and good making ourselves feel better about what we have, but doesn't all the poverty in the world prove that there isn't enough to go around?

Buckminster Fuller, perhaps the greatest practical philosopher of the 20th century and a fierce campaigner for ending world hunger, pointed out that we have enough resources for everyone in the world to live like a millionaire – we just don't have the belief that it's possible.

Part of the problem is that the field of economics is the study of society's allocation of 'scarce' resources. This presupposes that there's a fixed supply of resources in the world and how you divide them up is economics. Of course, we now know this is untrue, because technology is constantly changing what is scarce. It's no longer a question of limited resources, but of limited distribution.

According to the inspirational economist Professor Paul Zane Pilzer, 'Today, virtually 95 per cent of our economy is involved in producing products and services that did not exist fifty years ago, and the greatest economic opportunities of tomorrow are in sectors of our economy that do not even exist today.'

The more people there are buying and selling things to each other, the more money there has to be. Money is the oil in the machine of the world, and there has never been as much money flowing through the machinery as there is right now.

For example, we live in a world where so much money these days is created by computers – and computer chips are made from sand. It's because technology is the new determining factor in a country's wealth that nowadays even many traditional economists understand this:

The amount of money in the world is not limited – it's infinite.

Q. I'm confused! What if I'm not sure which beliefs are holding me back?

While here in the West confusion is generally considered to be a bad thing, in the East confusion is revered as the gateway to transformation and change. It's OK to be confused – it means that your old ideas are being challenged and space is being created for new ideas to form. Stick with it – by the time you finish this book, you will not only have more clarity, you will be experiencing more freedom, happiness and prosperity than before!

CHAPTER THREE

Reprogramming Your Wealth Thermostat

REPROGRAMMING YOUR WEALTH THERMOSTAT

The author Brandon Bays has been using the following scenario as part of an ongoing study into the psychology of wealth:

> *You have been shortlisted for a job for which you are well qualified. You interviewed well in the preceding rounds and are now one of the final five up for the job. Just before entering the final interview room you discover that the salary is not what you thought – it has an extra zero on it!*

> *In other words, the salary for the job is actually ten times more than you thought it was. If you thought it paid £30,000 a year, it turns out it really pays £300,000; if you had thought it paid £60,000 a year, you discover that it really pays £600,000.*

> *How would you feel as you were about to go in and face the interview panel? What would you do?*

What comes up for you as you imagine yourself in that room? For most people, it brings up all sorts of emotional issues ranging from unworthiness and worthlessness to overwhelm and even rage.

A number of people in the study wouldn't even go in for the final interview. A job that pays ten times more than they are used to earning is simply too far outside their comfort zone for them to even consider it.

The simple conclusion we can draw from this is that most people are carrying an unconscious 'upper limit' on how much money they would be comfortable earning. This makes sense, because our unconscious mind is a safety-seeking mechanism. Its number-one job is to keep you safe, and its primary way of doing this is to try to ensure that today is as much like yesterday as possible. From your unconscious mind's perspective, familiarity breeds safety.

In this way, your unconscious works much like a thermostat. If the thermostat is set for 70°, then the chances are that the temperature in the room is around 70°. If it started to get too much hotter, the air conditioning would kick it in and bring it back down into the 'comfort zone'.

Here's the key:

The only way to permanently change the temperature in the room is to reprogram the thermostat.

It's the same with money, success, fame or any other thing you may be pursuing in your life. The only way to permanently increase your wealth is to first reprogram your wealth thermostat!

Here are a few questions you can ask to give yourself a sense of where your internal thermostat is currently set. Unless you have experienced a radical change in fortunes over the past few months, these numbers will give you a fairly accurate sense of the amount of money you are currently comfortable having in your life.

TAKING YOUR FINANCIAL TEMPERATURE

1. How much money could you lose without freaking out? £5? £50? £500?

2. Look over your bank statements for the past 18 months or so. What's the average amount of money you've had in your account?

3. Add up the annual income and/or net worth of your five closest friends and divide by 5.

   Research suggests that your own income/net worth will be within 20 per cent of that number, which makes it a pretty good indication of where your thermostat is currently set.

A 'rich' thermostat

Most people live their lives on autopilot, doing things without really thinking about them. They listen to the same radio station, order the same food, and have the same kind of thoughts each day. Yet as the saying goes: 'If you keep doing what you've always done, you'll just get more of what you've already got.'

> *If you want to know the future, look at the past.*
>
> ALBERT EINSTEIN, Nobel Prize-winning physicist

If your thermostat is set low, that can be a problem. But what if it's already set for riches?

At one time, Donald Trump was over one billion dollars in debt. One of the bankers who was sent to demand their money back told me the story of how the meeting actually went. Despite the fact that they were there to shut him down, Trump welcomed them in style and set about persuading them to give him more time to get the money back. They agreed to let him try, but only if he was willing to put a tight leash on his spending.

Trump refused! He told them that if they wanted their money back, they were going to need to support him in the lifestyle to which he had become accustomed. He insisted on hundreds of thousands of dollars a month 'allowance' and full access to his private jets – in other words, to continue living his life on his own terms. Within a year, he had not only paid off the banks, he was also back to being hundreds of millions of dollars in profit.

His thermostat was set so high that it simply wouldn't allow him to have less than that for any appreciable period of time. Consequently, his mind was able to generate ways of quickly bringing that amount of money back into his life.

Similarly, nearly all of the rich thinkers I studied for this book told me that if they lost all their money tomorrow, they would have it back within a few years. This is why the difference between a rich thinker and a poor thinker can't be measured by the amount of money they have in the bank – it's the amount of money they can hold as natural and normal inside their minds.

There are numerous studies that show that people who come in to sudden massive wealth, be it through lottery wins or inheritance, are likely to get rid of it just as quickly. In fact, as many as 80 per cent of these people wind up being worse off financially within two years than they were before they received their windfall. Through a series of poor investments and unnecessary spending, the unconscious mind soon returns these people to their original levels of financial comfort.

If you want to avoid falling into this trap, it is important that before you go out and try to make a lot of money you make the space in your mind to hang on to it. In other words:

Until you actively reprogram your mind, your past will be an excellent indicator of your future.

Remember, your mind is like a computer, and throughout the course of this book, we are going to be changing it to make it easier and easier for you to notice where you are already rich, make more money and live a richer life.

Here's the first of a series of exercises I will guide you through in this chapter to reprogram your mind for greater wealth ...

IMAGINING UNLIMITED WEALTH

1. Think about how much money you have in the bank and notice what you imagine. Do you envision piles of bank notes, stacks of coins, a bank statement or something else?

2. Next, think about how much money you have coming in over the next year and again notice what comes to mind. Do you see cheques, notes, bank statements, envelopes, or numbers going up on your home computer?

3. Now, imagine double, triple or even quadruple the amount of money coming in. You might see more notes piling up, the figures on the cheques are bigger, or the numbers on the screen are increasing more quickly. Have fun with this!

4. Next, imagine that this flow of wealth increases every year for the next twenty years. Imagine stack after stack of bank notes being added to your account, making the piles bigger and bigger, or watching the numbers on your bank statement dramatically increase. Again, let your imagination run wild and enjoy it!

5. When you are done, let your mind settle on an image that feels expansive and rich to you, making sure that you always finish with more wealth in your mind than you had when you began.

It is essential that you allow yourself to enjoy this exercise! By stretching the limits of how much money you can imagine having, you are gradually resetting your wealth thermostat at a higher and higher level.

Cranking up the heat on your income

I have a friend who is a highly skilled corporate trainer who was convinced that he had reached the upper limit of what was acceptable to charge for his services. He was complaining to me that in order for him to make as much money as he wanted to make he would need to work 350 days a year, the thought of which was not only unpleasant to him but completely implausible as he'd never booked more than 50 training days in a single year before.

I asked him what he charged and he said £1,200 a day. So I strongly suggested to him that he add a zero to the very next proposal he sent out. He looked at me as though I was crazy. No matter how hard he tried, his brain simply couldn't comprehend the idea of being paid £12,000 for one day's work. After watching him struggle with this for a few moments, I said, 'OK, what if you just charged double what you used to? Worst case, they'll negotiate you back down to your normal day rate.'

I saw a smile begin to form on his face. 'I could do that,' he said.

Of course, had I suggested to him to double his day rate at the beginning, he would have found that difficult. But once the mind has been sufficiently stretched, it will never return to its original limitations. And once his mind had expanded to consider the possibility of earning £12,000 a day, only charging £2,400 a day not only felt easier, it felt like a relief from the exertion of trying to contemplate the larger number.

That is exactly the same thing we are going to do now. I am going to ask your brain to consider earning more money than you may have ever thought possible. Whether you are able to do this easily or not, practising in this way will open your mind to be able to consider larger and larger sums of money.

The pay-off for this is more than comfort. My friend not only got £2,400 a day for the training, he learned that his limitations about what is truly possible weren't real. The last time I spoke with him, he was regularly asking for and receiving £5,000 a day – and the number is still rising.

Here's a variation on what I did with my friend that you can do for yourself right now …

THE INCOME EXPANDER

1. Whatever you currently earn, imagine being paid double that for exactly the same amount of work.

2. When you can imagine that, double it again.

3. How high can you go? When you've reached the absolute upper limit of what you can currently imagine being paid, think about what else you could do for that money and see if you can make the number go up even higher.

4. When you really can't go any further, think about your current income and imagine increasing it by only 10 per cent. How possible does it feel?

Each time you repeat this exercise, you will find it easier and easier to imagine the changes and more and more comfortable to do so.

The power of focus revisited

Remember, one of the fundamental principles I laid out in the first chapter was this:

What you focus on, you get more of.

Psychological and scientific theory abounds as to why things work this way. Psychologists tend to explain it by talking about the reticular activating system, the part of your mind that enables you to filter out most of your environmental stimuli and only notice those things that seem relevant to your safety or highest values.

Behaviourists agree that you get more of what you focus on, but they explain it differently. They tend to assert that your beliefs and predominant emotional states matter only in as much as they affect your external behaviours; those behaviours in turn will create results in the world around you, creating a sort of a 'self-fulfilling prophecy' effect.

Scientists, particularly those interested in the field of quantum physics, have a different explanation, one made popular recently through the movie and book, *The Secret*.

The explanation is that everything in the universe – from our thoughts and language to our bodies and the physical world that surrounds us – is essentially made up of atoms and molecules vibrating at a particular energy frequency.

The basic rule of thumb when it comes to energy is sometimes known as the law of attraction:

Like attracts like.

The scientists who subscribe to this theory hold that our thoughts work like a magnet, and what we focus on consistently becomes 'attracted' to us. In music, this is called the principle of 'sympathetic resonance'. If you have two pianos in the same room and you hit a C note on one piano, you will find that the C string on the other piano will start vibrating at the same rate.

The emotions behind your thoughts determine the speed at which they manifest. You are broadcasting energy all the time. This is attracting and repelling things constantly. This is one reason why the richness of your thinking is ultimately more valuable than the size of your bank balance. Your thoughts are an energy that is both powerful and creative.

Whatever you choose to believe, what's important to remember is that focusing on what you lack will bring you more lack; focusing on expanding your thermostat and creating more money will bring you an expanded sense of possibility and greater wealth than ever before.

How did your thermostat get set?

> *Give me the boy and I will give you the man.*
>
> JEAN PIAGET,
> philosopher and scientist

Scientists have discovered that newly hatched chicks identify the first thing they see as their mother; they will form a bond with it and base their behaviours around it. This process is called 'imprinting', and researchers have done many experiments that have proved the power of conditioning at this formative stage of development.

The same is true to some extent with humans. The early experiences of your childhood shape you for later life. Your beliefs about money will be affected by the environment you grew up in and the attitudes of those around you. This is how you get 'programmed' to think about money in the way that you do.

Those early experiences act as a sort of 'training video' for your unconscious mind, and serve as either a warning or an example of what's possible. As a child you watch how the grown-ups around you handle money, and this sets up the potential for what you are capable of later in life.

For example, when I was growing up my father was in the construction business. Although he went through periods of great prosperity, the work was often erratic. I remember watching the enormous stress my parents were under as they rode this financial rollercoaster, and deciding as a child that I didn't ever want to have to worry about money. In fact, I wanted to make so much of it that it would never be an issue for me.

This was the early formation of my unconscious programming around money. But when I looked at how my own financial life was unfolding in my early thirties, I realized that deciding I wanted to have a lot of money was only part of what I'd learned.

Just like my father, I had fallen into the pattern of earning large sums of money and then getting rid of them. Although it felt like I was charting my own course, I was experiencing the exact same financial ups and downs as my parents. The only difference was, the ups were bigger – and so were the downs!

Once I recognized the pattern I was able to begin to change it, using the principle of hypnotic regression. Because people unconsciously act out of the patterns they learned in childhood, one of the most powerful techniques hypnotists use is to age regress their clients to a time before the limiting pattern was created. By exposing the unconscious mind to new patterns, people are then able to create a different set of filters on what's possible.

This leads us to an unusual-sounding conclusion:

It's never too late to have a wealthy childhood!

For example, one of my best friends went to Eton school and excelled in everything he did. I, on the other hand, went to an ordinary comprehensive school, and to say I did not achieve academic greatness in those early years is a bit of an understatement.

One day we were comparing the kind of messages we received about ourselves and our potential while at school. For as long as I can remember, I was told that nothing I did was good enough and that I should lower my sights and let go of any ambitions I had to make my mark upon the world. One of my school reports said that I 'would never amount to anything'. In sharp contrast, my friend was continually told that he was special and was 'a natural leader'.

Some of the differences were subtler. For example, a typical maths question at my school would be about how many apples and oranges you could buy for a pound if apples cost 20 pence and oranges cost 15 pence. One of the questions he remembered from his maths class began with the phrase, 'You are buying a small engineering company that has shown limited profitability in the first three years of operations …'

While we have both gone on to success in our chosen fields, my journey has been one of continual unlearning and reprogramming. His has been the natural and inevitable result of positive programming the first time around. What these differences made clear to me is that wherever your wealth thermostat is currently set, it's the natural and inevitable result of your childhood programming.

The experiences you had growing up and the messages you received about money, both consciously and unconsciously, created the blueprint for your current financial situation. We are about to change that blueprint for good.

Creating an alternative past

We are about to do one of the important techniques in this entire system. Strange though it may seem at first, this one technique alone can make all the difference in the world.

In a moment, we are going to create an alternative childhood for you – one where you grew up with all the advantages of being surrounded by rich thinkers who believed in you, believed in your potential and had the financial means to put that belief into practice.

This process will not take anything away from the childhood you actually had, and you will not forget anything important about your past. It is simply a way of providing your unconscious mind with some new alternatives, so you will no longer be constrained by the limits of your old wealth programming.

One important note
Some people had unhappy childhoods and find it uncomfortable
to think about them. Because we are imagining an alternative
childhood, you do not need to think about the one you actually had
to successfully complete this exercise. If you feel any discomfort,
simply stop and only return to it later when you are ready.

I am now going to ask you to close your eyes and vividly imagine having had richer life. The more detail you are willing to go into, the more impact the exercise will have. Keep experimenting with it until you really get a strong sense of exactly what it would have been like ...

YOUR WEALTHY CHILDHOOD

Read all the way though the exercise first so you know exactly what to do. Then when you're ready, go back through, really taking the time to imagine each scenario in great detail.

1. Imagine being born into a wonderful home where, from the moment you enter the world, you absolutely know that you are loved, you are wanted and there will always be enough – a truly rich environment.

2. What is it like to be a small child knowing that wherever you go and whatever you do, you are loved, wanted and there is always enough? What kinds of presents would you get for your birthday? What kinds of friends would you play with? What kinds of positive messages and advice do you receive in this rich environment? What kinds of beliefs do you form about what's possible growing up in this rich world?

3. What would it be like to be a teenager having grown up knowing that from the moment you were born there was always enough money to do whatever you truly wanted to do? Who would you want to hang out with? Where would you want to travel to? What kind of hopes and dreams might you have for your future? How secure and confident do you feel?

4. How about as you are making the transition to adulthood – what kinds of things do you want to do? Who do you want to do them with? Where do you choose to live? How do you feel about yourself? How do you feel about life, knowing that no matter what happens there will always be enough?

5. What kinds of things are you drawn to in your twenties?

6. In your thirties?

7. In your forties?

8. In your fifties?

9. In your sixties?

10. In your seventies?

What is it like to grow old having spent a lifetime knowing that you were loved, wanted and have always had enough money to do whatever you wanted to do? What have you learned?

If you like, you can write your answers as though you are writing your autobiography. For example:

In my twenties, I realized that because I had such a privileged upbringing, I had a responsibility to give back to the world in whatever way I could. While I continued to do the work I love in the art world and run my businesses, I also began advising and ultimately contributing large sums of money to charities that focused on offering education as well as financial support to young people.

As I grew older, I knew I might lose touch with what it was like to have the whole of my life ahead of me, so I wanted to support organizations that could get to people before life had a chance to knock the hope out of them ...

While this is just an imagination exercise, every single person I have guided through it has noticed tangible changes in their lives, often within just a few days. You can reinforce your learning each time you listen to the hypnosis CD.

FREQUENTLY ASKED QUESTIONS ABOUT 'REPROGRAMMING YOUR WEALTH THERMOSTAT'

Q. I think my thermostat is set too high! I can't bear the thought of taking a job that only pays minimum wage, so I've been on unemployment for ages.

If you're wondering where your thermostat is set, you need look no further than your income and bank balance. If you're consistently not earning any money, it doesn't matter what your explanation is – your thermostat is set for 'no money'.

Practising the exercises in this chapter will make you more and more comfortable having money in your life – and if you allow yourself some time to proceed with the ideas and exercises in this book, you'll find you can gradually increase your income without any undue stress or discomfort.

Q. All this programming and reprogramming sounds dangerous. Is it really safe to do this?

I have purposely chosen only to include those exercises in this book that I have tested with hundreds and sometimes thousands of people in private sessions and public workshops. Simply follow the instructions as I lay them out and you will find them not only safe but remarkably effective.

If you are really concerned about a particular exercise, simply give that one a miss until you're ready. So long as you continue to listen to the hypnosis CD on a regular basis, the system will work for you!

CHAPTER FOUR

Overcoming Emotional Spending

OVERCOMING EMOTIONAL SPENDING

The difference between rich people and poor people is that poor people spend their money and then save what's left; rich people save their money and spend what's left.

JIM ROHN,
motivational speaker

When I first started working with the ideas in this system, I began to earn far more money than I had ever imagined possible. In my first year, I brought in more money than I'd ever dreamed of having. What shocked me was that when my tax bill came due, I didn't have enough left in my account to pay it!

That's when I realized that I had only mastered half of the equation. While making money is a wonderful skill, accumulating a surplus of that money is an important part of nearly every rich thinker's plan for a lifetime of riches.

Which brings us to an important question:

Do you get more pleasure from spending money or accumulating it?

While either pattern taken to an extreme can become a problem, everyone has a tendency towards either spending money as it comes in or seeking to keep it. Those patterns are often set in childhood, when extra money brought in through allowances, birthday presents and summer jobs was either saved up in a piggy bank or immediately spent down the shops on a Saturday afternoon.

Whatever your current programming, in this chapter I am going to teach you how to put money back into your pocket without budgeting and without feeling deprived. You will not only spend less money, you'll get more value for the money you do spend. Soon, you will begin to accumulate a surplus of wealth – and that surplus will provide the basis for your financial future.

The joy of saving

> *Given a big enough 'why', people can bear almost any 'how'.*
>
> FRIEDRICH NIETZSCHE, philosopher

People sometimes ask me if I recommend they use any available money to pay off debt or increase savings when they are beginning a program to create more money in their life. While everyone is different and it is important to honour your debts, I always encourage them to take at least a portion of that available money and use it to begin accumulating some savings.

There are two reasons for this, both of which are psychologically and scientifically proven:

1. The more you have, the less susceptible you are to the emotional rollercoaster of financial life.

Imagine for a moment that you have £10 in savings and you lose £1 – how do you feel?

Now imagine that you have £100 and you lose that same £1 – does it feel different? What if you had £1,000? £10,000? £1,000,000?

Similarly, imagine making an extra £100 today – how would that make you feel?

Would you feel the same way if you already had £1,000 in the bank? £10,000? £1,000,000?

When we have money in the bank, it's easier to avoid the

emotional highs and lows of profit and loss, which in turn allows you to practise your rich thinking and make smart financial decisions from within the money zone.

2. The more you have, the more you get.

Have you ever noticed that the rich often seem to get richer? Because they already have money, their unconscious mind spends its time searching for ways to create even more of it. And because your unconscious is at work 24 hours a day, it will find exactly what it's looking for.

> *Compound interest is the eighth wonder of the world.*
>
> ALBERT EINSTEIN, Nobel Prize-winning physicist

Remember our basic rule of thumb:

What you focus on, you get more of.

In this sense, money in the bank acts like a magnet for more money. Not only will you benefit over time from the compounding effect of interest, you will also benefit from the compounding effect of focus.

Now, if you're thinking you couldn't possibly save money on your income, that's just some poor thinking from an old program in your mind. You don't need to earn one extra penny to begin building your 'money magnet'. As you learn and apply the techniques for overcoming emotional spending I will share with you in this chapter, you will naturally and effortlessly spend less money. Then use that money to begin your savings plan. Here is a simple exercise you can do that will turbo-charge your intention to accumulate wealth. It will begin changing the perceptual filters of your mind even as you do it.

THE VALUE OF SAVINGS

Do this exercise quickly – it doesn't matter if you think all your answers are 'good ones' …

1. Make a list of 50 things you would love to do, be or have in your life if only you had more money in the bank.

   Example:

   A nicer car

   More holiday time

   Learn to fly a plane

   Move to the country

2. Now, make a list of 50 ways that having more money would help you achieve your highest values.

   Example:

   More time with my family

   Able to contribute to my favourite causes

   I would be less stressed and as a result, more patient

3. Circle any items on your lists that are particularly motivating to you. You can put reminders by your computer or write them on the inside cover of your chequebook to remind you of what you are postponing each time you spend money on something trivial in the moment.

Building a 'money magnet' provides you with a cushion of wealth that makes it easier to sustain rich thinking and provides you with the funds to invest in developing your business, product or service. So why don't we all make accumulating wealth our top priority?

The answer may surprise you ...

How we are programmed to spend

In 1923, Montgomery Ward and several other wealthy US retailers hired a man named Edward Bernays to advise them on how to boost sales in a flagging post-WW1 economy. Bernays was the nephew of Sigmund Freud, and he taught them to link the purchase of goods and services to people's ego needs – sex, status, prestige, and a sense of themselves as prosperous and successful.

Up until that time, most people bought things for practical purposes – if you had a pair of trousers, you wouldn't buy another one until the first pair wore out. But Bernays reframed that behaviour from a virtue into a vice. If someone felt they couldn't afford or didn't need the clothes, the sales people were taught to make that person feel insignificant and unworthy. On the other hand, buying the 'right' brand of clothes, watch or car would let everyone know that you were sophisticated, rich, successful or a worthy mate, even though logically everyone knew the connection was completely made up.

At the time, this radical new approach fuelled both the boom of post-war prosperity in the 1920s and the subsequent depression of the 1930s. And nowadays the techniques advertisers use are far more advanced and far more subtle. The consumer culture all around us offers us an overwhelming number of ways to get an instant burst of good feelings.

A bit down today? Buy these shoes and chase the blues away!

Not feeling great about yourself? Those jeans might do the trick!

Feeling like you're working harder than ever without getting ahead? You deserve a new car!

And it is not just the clothes, the toys and the status symbols – it is the brands too. Notice how you feel when you say each one of these famous brand names inside your mind:

- Porsche
- Valentino
- Louis Vuitton
- Rolls Royce
- Ralph Lauren

Every brand is an emotional trigger. Vast sums of money are spent through advertising and in all sorts of other more subtle ways to ensure that when you see a brand, or a crucial design element associated with it, particular emotions are triggered in you.

Very often it is done so subtly and elegantly that you don't even notice it happening. But, let me assure you, it is still happening. In fact, so many advertising executives used to show up on our hypnosis trainings that I now consider teaching people how the mind *really* works is a kind of 'consumer protection for the brain'.

In one famous study, men who saw a new car advertisement that included a seductive young woman rated the car as faster, more appealing, more expensive-looking and better designed than men who viewed the same ad without the model. Yet when asked later the men refused to believe that the presence of a model had influenced their judgement.

These days there are so many brands that are linked to prestige, sex and success in our culture that we don't even question the association. Combine this with the ready availability of credit, and the constant bombardment of advertising messages on an unprepared mind can be extremely costly.

The real cost of 'retail therapy'

Have you ever gone shopping to cheer yourself up?

While there is nothing wrong in theory with 'retail therapy', if you can't stop yourself or you are continually buying things you don't use or need, you are out of control. What was once a way of

> *Shoppers go into a store to buy something; shopaholics go into a store to see if there is anything to buy.*
>
> MICHAEL NEILL,
> success coach

'taking the edge off' can become a full-blown addiction.

This is what happened to a client of mine whose shopping 'habit' had got completely out of control. Even though she knew she was spending a fortune on things she never used, she felt helpless in the face of a new dress or a 10 per cent discount.

Well-meaning friends would say to her that she should just 'get a grip on herself' or 'stop being so stupid', but try as she might she couldn't stop herself. Despite her well-paid job, she was haemorrhaging money. When I met her she was just a few months away from losing her home and being out on the streets with her young daughter.

How can something as seemingly innocent as shopping create the same devastating impact as the excessive use of alcohol or drugs?

The eminent researcher Dr Ronald Ruden has made a fascinating study of how we are addicted to happy brain chemicals such as serotonin. We can get these from any number of things: a compliment, our favourite TV show, our football team winning, sharing a conversation with like-minded people. Also from sex, drink, drugs, gambling ... and shopping.

When we buy something we like or we think will enhance us in some way we release a happy chemical in our brains called serotonin. But as with almost any drug, the more you take, the more you need to take to get the same level of release.

Many of the things we purchase we are buying in order to make ourselves feel differently. Of course, there's nothing wrong with having good feelings about a purchase. However, if that's your favourite way of getting good feelings, it could prove expensive.

Because my client had so many bad feelings floating around inside her body (following two separate traumas she had suffered), she was desperate to find something that would ease her pain. And as with most of us, the first place she looked was outside herself. Since she 'wasn't the kind of person' who would get involved with gambling or drugs, she turned to something else – shopping.

Fortunately, once you recognize that you are stuck in a self-defeating pattern of behaviour, it is relatively easy to break free. Overcoming any addiction is ultimately a matter of reprogramming ourselves, changing our associations, our biochemistry, and then our actions.

There are two main things you need to do:

1. Change your old associations.
2. Redesign your priorities.

1. Change your old associations

The biggest expense my client had was designer clothes. Whenever she was feeling down she would head down to her favourite shops, 'just to look'. Because she was such a 'loyal, valuable customer', the shop assistants would treat her like a princess, though it was more likely they were too busy counting their impending commissions to really be paying much attention to her.

She would look around the shop for as long as possible, working her feelings up into a frenzy and getting high on the anticipation of the purchase. Then, when she was good and ready, she would whip out her credit card and satisfy her craving. By the time she left the shop, she didn't even care about what she had bought and her home was overflowing with unopened packages.

In order to shatter her old associations, I asked her to think of her favourite designer labels, Missoni and Gucci. Then, I had her create an associational link to them by asking her to squeeze the thumb and forefinger together. We repeated this process several times until just squeezing her fingers together would bring up her clothing lust.

Next, I asked her think of something she would never want to buy – crack cocaine. As she thought about this unpleasant notion, we built up her sense of repulsion more and more until she looked quite nauseous. I then had her once again squeeze her thumb and finger together, this time at the very height of the repulsion, collapsing the old, pleasant associations. Within a few minutes, I had linked those feelings of repulsion directly to her favourite designer labels. Her ability to shop without thinking as a way to get good feelings had begun to change for ever.

Here is a variation on this same exercise you can do for yourself…

FROM LUST TO DISGUST

Before you do this technique for yourself, read through each step so that you know exactly what to do.

1. Think of your favourite 'emotional purchase' – the thing you are most likely to buy in order to cheer yourself up or feel better about yourself.

2. As you think about it, put the thumb and forefinger of your **left hand** together. Repeat this several times with as many different emotional purchases as you can think of until just squeezing those fingers together begins to bring up some of that 'shopping lust'.

3. Now, think of something that you would never buy, no matter what. It might be a handgun that had been used in a murder, a piece of extreme pornography or a Nazi flag. The more outraged and disgusted you are at the mere thought of it, the better.

4. As you continue to imagine that awful purchase, double the image in your mind's eye so that it almost overwhelms you. When you are truly uncomfortable, once again squeeze together the thumb and finger of your **left hand**.

5. Repeat this process as many times as you need until the very idea of buying those things leaves you with a feeling of discomfort. The more distasteful an item you can think of in step 3, the faster and more powerfully this technique will work for you.

Of course, if all we did was make her feel bad about what she used to get pleasure from, she would simply substitute some other external means to get her fix. So I needed to teach her to get the happy feelings she used to get from shopping in other ways.

I asked her to vividly remember times she had experienced great pleasure and happiness and squeeze the thumb and middle finger of her right hand together. She remembered the moment she first held her baby in her arms, times she'd laughed with friends and other moments involving pleasure of a more personal nature.

Soon, she only had to squeeze her thumb and middle finger together and she would feel good. Once we had created this 'feel good button', I asked her to think of some of the situations that in the past had sent her off to the shops. Each time she thought about one, she would squeeze her thumb and finger together and fire off the good feeling while imagining doing something else instead.

After repeated practice, she could imagine going about her daily life without the overwhelming compulsion to shop. We had linked negative feelings to the thought of buying unnecessary and expensive items, and positive feelings to her everyday life.

Now it's your turn ...

We are now going to program your mind and body to release happy chemicals without shopping so that you automatically experience good feelings at times when you used to feel the need to shop. This will not only reset your body's natural balance, it will also enable you to feel good whenever you want without the use of shopping, alcohol, cigarettes, food or any other artificial stimulants.

We will do this by adding a stack of positive feelings to the 'rich anchor' you created in chapter one. So in a moment, I am going to ask you to remember some times in your life when you felt particularly good without shopping. Then we are going to create an association between those feelings and this squeeze of your fingers by repeating them together, over and over again.

Ready? Here we go ...

THE FEEL-GOOD BUTTON

Before you do this technique for yourself, read through each step so that you know exactly what to do.

1. Press the thumb and middle finger of your **right hand** together to fire off the 'rich anchor' you created in chapter one.

2. Now, remember a time you felt really, really good – you were having fun with friends, someone paid you a compliment, you felt incredibly loved. Return to it as though you are back there now. Remember that time vividly – see what you saw, hear what you heard and feel how good you felt.

3. As you keep going through that memory again and again, continue to squeeze your thumb and middle finger together on your right hand. Notice all the details, and make the images bigger and the colours richer, bolder and brighter. Make the sounds louder and crisper and the feelings stronger.

4. Next, think of a time that you felt DEEP PLEASURE. It needs to be intense and strong. As you keep going through that memory again and again, squeeze your thumb and middle finger together on your **right** hand. Recall it as vividly as possible. Remember that time, see what you saw, hear what you heard and feel how good you felt.

5. OK, stop and relax. You'll know you've done this correctly when you squeeze your thumb and finger together and you feel that good feeling again. Go ahead, do that now – just squeeze thumb and finger together and enjoy feeling these wonderful feelings.

6. Now imagine taking that good feeling with you into all the situations where in the past you would have felt the compulsion to go shopping. See what you'll see and hear what you'll hear as you take that good feeling in to each one of those situations without any need to buy anything at all.

7. Take yourself through a few difficult situations and handle each one of them perfectly. Here are a few examples:

   • You are at work and it's a little stressful, but you are able to deal with it easily.

   • You're sitting home alone and you're feeling bored. You know your paycheque has just hit your bank account, and you're wondering what to do. You fire off your rich anchor and begin to smile. It occurs to you that you haven't seen one of your good friends for some time, and you arrange a time to meet.

Imagine each scenario again and again until you feel really good about your ability to manage your own feelings without having to spend money to do so.

2. Redesign your priorities

At this point, my client became a bit concerned that she'd never be able to shop again. The reality, as I pointed out to her, is that she hadn't lost anything – she had gained the ability to make wise choices about how she used her money.

In order to reinforce that point, I asked her to make three very important lists. Her 'A' list would consist of essential items that she must buy each week, like food for her and the baby. Her 'B' list included items that were important but not essential, such as paying her mobile phone bill and saving to build a financial cushion. Everything else went on the 'C' list.

From now on she would buy only 'A' list items first, then distribute her money on 'B' list items when there was money left over. Until she began to build her financial cushion, 'C' list items wouldn't get bought at all.

How well did it work? Within a few short months her entire life had changed. She was climbing out of debt, feeling good about herself and saving money to invest in her future.

Even though your spending may not be out of control, everybody can benefit from this exercise.

ABC LIST EXERCISE

1. Write down a list of everything that you currently spend money on, from groceries to your mortgage to family holidays.

2. Assign an 'A', 'B' or 'C' to each expense.

   A = essential

   B = important, but not essential

   C = everything else

3. In future, spend money on the As and Bs first.

Every time you are thinking about spending money in the future, consider which list the expense should be on and make your decision accordingly!

An end to 'money diets'

> *When people use credit cards, they are often spending money they don't have on things they don't need to impress people they don't even like.*
>
> — TAVIS SMILEY,
> journalist and political commentator

Most systems of dieting and budgeting are based on punishment and reward. If you're 'good' – that is, you deny yourself food and/or shopping for a set period of time – you get a treat. If you're 'bad', you don't get the treat, plus you're supposed to feel bad about what you've done.

But here's the problem:

Diets don't work!

While systematically starving yourself can keep the pounds off in the short term, over time nearly everyone winds up putting the weight back on, often bouncing back to a higher weight than ever before.

This is the same experience nearly everyone who tries to put themselves on a tight, restrictive budget is up against, and the reason 'money diets' rarely work for more than about 90 days.

Here's one last technique you can use, regardless of your current spending habits, which will take advantage of your inner wisdom by slowing down the spending process so that you can no longer do so unconsciously. While you can certainly adapt the technique to meet your needs, do it exactly as written in order to get the maximum benefits.

GROWING YOUR FINANCIAL AWARENESS

1. For the next thirty days, put your credit cards away somewhere safe. You are going to be spending on a 'cash-only' basis.

2. Before you buy anything, ask yourself a question that will heighten your consciousness around what you are about to spend. Some of my favourites include:

   - Is this an 'A', 'B' or a 'C'?

     A = essential

     B = important, but not essential

     C = everything else

   - Do I really want this or do I just want to feel better?

   - Will spending money on this make me richer or poorer?

3. Immediately after buying something, take out your notebook and write down exactly what you spent, from 30 pence for a packet of crisps to £30 for petrol.

On average, following these three steps will add less than a minute to your purchase time, but I have seen it cut down the amount people spend by as much as 50 per cent!

As you apply these techniques, you will be amazed at how much money you begin to save without even trying. By using these savings to fund your 'money magnet', your wealth will grow by leaps and bounds!

FREQUENTLY ASKED QUESTIONS ABOUT 'OVERCOMING EMOTIONAL SPENDING'

Q. I've read that I should just stop drinking coffee and use the extra money to become rich. Is this the same idea?

One of the most talked-about ideas in popular finance today is what bestselling American author David Bach calls 'the latte factor'. The idea is that if you cut out the equivalent of one latte a day, the money you save would be sufficient to launch your financial campaign to begin an investment pro-gramme, which over a twenty-year period would make you a millionaire.

While this is not an inherently bad idea, when you learn to identify and stop your emotional spending, you will likely save tens of thousands of pounds a year. As a bonus, you can drink all the coffee you like!

Q. Are credit cards really as big a problem as the top financial advisers make them out to be?

If anything, they're an even bigger problem. Studies have conclusively shown that people spend more when they pay using credit cards. More surprisingly, *merely having the credit card symbols on display in the shop will create greater sales.* Perhaps this is the reason that, at the time of writing, credit-card debt in the UK has reached a staggering £53.4 billion pounds!

Our society has gone a bit spending-mad, but that doesn't mean you have to go into consumer debt in order to live rich. A friend of mine taught me a fun little game to play where you see how many different ways you are invited by television, advertising, stores, newspapers and magazines to go deeper into debt each day.

Here's a list to get you started:

- No Money Down
- No Payments
- Operators are standing by
- Here's your pre-approved credit card
- Bad credit – no problem!
- Send no money now
- Buy now, pay later

This doesn't mean you can't ever make use of consumer credit. But switching to a 'cash-only' spending policy in the short term can save you a surprising amount of money – and that money can be used to begin providing you with the financial cushion you so richly deserve.

Q. I play the lottery every week, and occasionally win as much as £100. Surely spending £10 a week on lottery tickets is a better investment than just sticking that money in a savings account, isn't it?

Let's get really real for a moment – your chances of winning the lottery are 14 million to one.

If you're going to gamble on anything, gamble on yourself. £10 a week becomes £500 a year – and with the additional savings you'll make as you overcome your emotional spending habits, you'll accumulate a healthy financial cushion before you know it.

CHAPTER FIVE

Tapping into the Flow of Wealth

TAPPING INTO THE FLOW OF WEALTH

Do you know that amazing state when time seems to slow down and you are able to do and say just the right things at just the right moment? A challenge arises and you handle it perfectly. You are thinking clearly and easily in a relaxed, alert state of clarity and focus.

Athletes refer to this experience as being in 'the zone'; musicians refer to it as playing in 'the groove'; psychologists call it living in 'the flow'. Scientific research studies into this amazing state show us that everyone experiences it, although some more than others. Indeed many people go out of their way to experience it, taking on sporting challenges or indeed doing any activity because of the 'buzz' or the 'high' they get from it.

When you are in the zone, you do what you do better, with a greater sense of ease and mastery. If you get into that state when you are focused on creating wealth, you'll not only find the ideas begin to flow, you'll find yourself enjoying the process more and more. Please note that I am not suggesting there won't be any effort involved – just that there doesn't have to be a sense of struggle.

What most people don't realize is that the experience of being 'in the zone' is a neuro-physiological state. In other words, the flow state is the result of a chemical and electrical change that happens inside you, and therefore you can learn to trigger it more and more of the time.

Here's a simple exercise that with practice will enable you to create this state any time you choose.

CREATING FLOW

Read all the way through this exercise before you begin ...

1. Stop for a moment and vividly remember a time you were in the zone, doing something you love and loving doing it. It might have been painting, playing tennis, driving, giving a presentation, telling funny stories with friends, designing something. What you were doing doesn't matter – what matters is how you felt when you were doing it. Any activity you were engaged in where you felt that peak state of flow is perfect.

2. Keep going through that memory again and again and again until you begin to feel that sense of being in the flow.

3. When you do, add that feeling into your rich anchor by putting your thumb and middle finger together on your right hand.

4. Now, continue to hold your newly enhanced rich anchor. While you are feeling rich and in the zone, imagine all the different ways you can make money. See yourself handling any challenges that arise and experience everything flowing perfectly!

The more you practise the exercise on page 111, the more familiar you will become with living in the flow. The more you live in and work in flow states, the easier your life will become.

So why don't we all live in flow all of the time?

When it comes to money, the answer is more in our biology than our psychology ...

The biochemistry of fear and greed

Have you ever wondered why no matter how much people have they always seem to want more?

Although the quest for more, bigger and better is so inherent in our culture that most people never question it, there is in fact a biological basis for our drive to succeed.

> *Money is neither my God nor my devil. It is a form of energy which tends to make us more of who we are, whether it's greedy or loving.*
>
> DAN MILLMAN,
> writer

Here's how it works:

Whenever we see something we want, our brain releases a neuro-transmitter into our bloodstream called 'dopamine'. This release of dopamine creates the feeling of craving in our bodies, as if we 'have to have' whatever it is that we want.

Then, when we actually achieve our desired end result and get what we want, our brains reward us with the 'feel good' neuro-transmitter called 'serotonin'. The interplay between these two chemical messengers in our body is going on all day, every day. We are continually moving between desire and the achievement of our desire, and the whole game is regulated by our brain chemistry.

When we are watching a football match, as the ball goes up and down the field we release more and more dopamine, building a craving inside our bodies for our team to score a goal. When they do, our brains release serotonin into our blood stream and we feel fantastic!

The exact same process comes into play when we engage in the pursuit of making money. As our desire to close a deal builds, so does the release of brain chemicals. This is why some of the wealthiest people in the world continue to work as if their life depended on it – they feel compelled to do so because they're actually chemically addicted to the feeling of success!

This is why it is so important to find work that you enjoy doing and is aligned with your highest values. If your good feelings in life come only from making money and doing deals, you will wind up pursuing money like a commodity. No matter how much you have, it will never feel like enough.

On the other hand, there are some people who pursue money as a substitute for a feeling of security. They are the ones who feel like they always need a little bit more to be 'safe'. In this case, the quest for more is driven by the fear of 'not enough' – not enough love, not enough self-esteem and not enough good feelings. And all the money in the world can't fill a hole that's psychological, not physical.

Again, unless we actively step in and take control, our brain chemistry runs the show. In this case, the adrenaline of fear drives the pursuit of money, and the serotonin of success temporarily soothes the fear. It feels so good to get that burst of good feelings that people will literally scare themselves into going out and making even more money, and the cycle continues.

Are you addicted to money?

I have a friend who is conservatively worth over £150 million pounds. Despite his ongoing business success, his first thought when he wakes up in the morning is: Will today be the day that I lose it all?

Remember, this is more than just a book about making money. I have seen more than a few people who come from an impoverished background make a lot of money in the pursuit of good feelings, but ultimately that kind of money never brings them happiness. Until they change their wealth programming they too will never feel like they have enough.

The point is this:

If you treat money like a drug,
you are likely to become an addict.

If you feel like you have to have more money in order to relax and feel good, you are out of control and money is in charge of your life. No matter how much money you accumulate, you will never be rich!

In just a few moments, we are going to turn that pattern around. Simply follow my instructions and you will find yourself back in control!

Getting back into the flow of wealth

Rich thoughts lead to rich feelings, and the richer you feel the richer your life becomes. In order to create greater possibilities in your thinking, it is highly useful to think about money from a place of ease and flow.

The people I have met who I consider to be truly rich are those who live predominantly in the flow, using their wealth as an expression of their deepest values. Because they are not addicted to money, they are able to use it as a simple tool to create more of what they want in their lives.

The exercise I am about to share with you may seem a bit strange, but it will enable you to quickly and easily let go of both your fear of not having enough money and your craving to have even more. It will make it easier and easier for you to relate to money as a simple tool – a way of facilitating the pursuit of what you really want to be, do and have in your life.

You are going to learn how to eliminate your fear and greed around money. This will not diminish your motivation to make or to have it. You will still keep all of your drive and focus, but you will no longer feel out of control or be at the mercy of your feelings. Instead of having to ride the emotional rollercoaster of fear or greed when it comes to money, you will be able to stay balanced and centred in the flow of wealth.

The technique we are about to do involves tapping on acupuncture points while you imagine being fearful or lustful around money. This will have the effect of de-sensitizing these negative emotional states (fear and greed) that you have linked to money, and creating a greater sense of balance, peace and neutrality. By the time you have finished the exercise, you will be firmly centred in 'the money zone'.

DEALING WITH FEAR

Read all the way through this exercise before you begin ...

1. Imagine having lost all your money, and rate your fear on a scale of 1 to 10 with 1 being the lowest and 10 the highest. This rating is essential, because in a few moments we will want to know how much better it's become.

2. As you focus in, imagine being completely broke, feel the fear and take two fingers of either hand and tap about ten times under your collarbone.

3. Now tap under your eye ten times.

4. Now tap under your collarbone again.

5. Place your other hand in front of you and tap on the back of it between your ring finger and your little finger. Continue to concentrate on the fear as you do this and each of the steps that follow: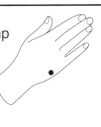

   • Close your eyes and open them.

   • Keep your head still, keep tapping and look down to the right then down to the left.

   • Keep tapping and rotate your eyes round 360 degrees clockwise, and now 360 degrees anti-clockwise.

   Remember to keep thinking about the fear of having absolutely no money as you do this!

   • Now hum the first few lines of 'Happy Birthday' out loud.

   • Count out loud from 1 to 5.

   • Once again hum the first few lines of 'Happy Birthday' out loud.

6. Stop and check – on a scale from 1 to 10, what number is your fear at now? Keep doing this until your fear is down to a 2 or 1.

At this point, you can either take a break or move straight on to the next exercise …

DEALING WITH LUST AND GREED

Read all the way through this exercise before you begin …

1. Now imagine having unlimited wealth – more money than you could possibly spend in several lifetimes. Feel the desire well up within you and rate your lust and greed on a scale of 1 to 10.

2. As you focus in, imagine having massive amounts of money and all the things you can buy with it, and allow the feelings of lust and greed to come up to the surface. When you're really feeling it, take two fingers of either hand and tap about ten times under your collarbone.

3. Now tap under your eye ten times.

4. Now tap under your collarbone again.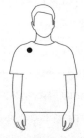

5. Place your other hand in front of you and tap on the back of it between your ring finger and your little finger. Continue to concentrate on the lust and greed as you do this and each of the steps that follow: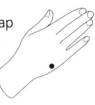

- Close your eyes and open them.
- Keep your head still, keep tapping and look down to the right then down to the left.
- Keep tapping and rotate your eyes round 360 degrees clockwise, and now 360 degrees anti-clockwise.

Remember to keep thinking about the massive amounts of money you were craving as you do this!

- Now hum the first few lines of 'Happy Birthday' out loud.
- Count out loud from 1 to 5.
- Once again hum the first few lines of 'Happy Birthday' out loud.

6. Stop and check – on a scale from 1 to 10, what number is your lust and greed down to now? Repeat the tapping sequence until it's down to a 2 or 1.

You may need to repeat this exercise several times in order to clear any residual fear or greed out of your system. You will know that you are done when you can think about not having money or having all the money in the world with a wonderful feeling of peace and ease. Welcome back to the zone!

FREQUENTLY ASKED QUESTIONS ABOUT 'TAPPING INTO THE FLOW OF WEALTH'

Q. This feels a bit like 'cheating'. Shouldn't flow be something spontaneous, that either happens or it doesn't?

Historically, flow states were thought of as mystical experiences that either happened or they didn't. Artists and poets would invoke the muse and then sit around drinking wine and waiting for her to show up before they began creating.

Here in the 21st century, we live in an age of leading-edge psychological technology. Because we are so much more aware of how our brains really work, we have more control than ever before. In fact, our understanding of psychology and biochemistry has progressed further in the past 30 years than it had in the previous 300 years.

Poor thinkers may bemoan the 'loss of innocence', but in a few years we'll look back on the idea of waiting for flow to happen the way you probably think about ancient rituals. And the state of the art continues to progress. Soon, designer drugs and mind machines will allow anyone to access the kinds of neuro-physiological states that used to be the exclusive preserve of yogis and mystics. And our increased control over the power of the mind makes us more stable, more functional and considerably happier.

Q. I feel really flat after doing the fear and greed exercise. I think I understand getting rid of the fear, but what's wrong with being excited about making lots of money?

There's nothing wrong with being excited about making money, but when you get consumed by it, your thinking process becomes corrupted. You start to equate your rich feelings with your bank balance instead of recognizing that 'rich' is a state of mind and a quality of being.

The Buddhists talk about it in terms of attachments and aversions. Suffering doesn't come from things or conditions – it comes from our attachment or aversion to them. By eliminating both the fear *and* the greed – that is, the aversion *and* the attachment – you become free. You may still have a lot of money and stuff, but that money and stuff no longer has you.

Q. That really seemed to work for me. Am I really 'cured'?

Despite everything we have discussed here, I guarantee that there will be times when you once again get caught up in both fearful, scarcity thinking and greedy, lustful thinking. When you do, stop. Don't beat yourself up and don't try to 'push through it'. Simply repeat the tapping exercise as necessary and get yourself back into the flow!

CHAPTER SIX

Creating a Rich Vision

CREATING A RICH VISION

> *To achieve great success in business you have to have an outrageously rich vision.*
>
> SOL KERZNER,
> billionaire hotelier

Several years ago I took part in a twenty-year reunion at one of the first radio stations I ever worked at. At one point in the evening, the former managing director of the station came over to me and with a smile handed me a folded-up, crinkled piece of paper with handwriting on it. This is what it said:

I will be a millionaire by the age of 30!

Just below that was my signature. Suddenly it all came back to me. Some years ago, I was having a 'creative difference' with that managing director. It's fair to say I was a rather cocky young man, and I got into a prolonged discussion in which I told him how I knew best and how hugely successful I was going to be. In the midst of the argument, I declared to him that I would be a millionaire by the time I was thirty.

Even I was surprised at the boldness of my declaration, but he just laughed and said, 'We'll see – let's have a sportsman's bet.' I wrote it down on the piece of paper and signed it – the same piece of paper he had kept and showed me that night.

I was indeed a millionaire by thirty, but not just because I wrote it down. I became a millionaire because for the next ten years I imagined it from every angle, over and over and over again.

While not all the rich thinkers I spoke to in putting together this book had clearly written goals, they did have one thing in common – a rich, clear vision of what they wanted to create in their lives and in the world.

So ... what do you want?

I remember asking one client to imagine that it was one year from now and she had had the best year of her life. When I asked her what was different, she said, 'I have a new carpet in my living room.' Her limited vision was a symptom of her impoverished model of the world. I explained to her that your life can only become as rich as you are willing to imagine it. I also asked her a bigger question:

What would you do if you knew you couldn't fail?

I encouraged her to let her mind run wild and think outside of the limits of her current comfort zone. 'After all,' I pointed out, 'it takes the same amount of energy to visualize a parking space as it does to visualize a beautiful new car to go in it!'

This time, she came back with a truly rich vision of what her life could become if she was willing to cultivate the vision and take action.

So ... if you could only succeed, what would you go for?

Do not underestimate the power of your creative mind! Remember, every great scientific innovation, medical miracle, song, painting, movie, poem and political movement started as just an idea in someone's creative imagination. The richer your thoughts, the more powerfully creative your imagination gets to be.

A valuable distinction

When I work with a client, the first and most important question I ask is: 'What do you want?' Whether they answer 'to quit smoking' or 'to lose weight' or 'to earn a million pounds', the next question I ask is always the same:

> *You have 50,000 thoughts a day – you might as well make them big ones.*
>
> DONALD TRUMP,
> billionaire entrepreneur

What do you want it for?

People want what they want for a variety of reasons. Some people want to have money because they think it will give them 'security'; others want it because they think it will buy them 'freedom'. Still others want a sense of 'power' or 'achievement' or 'success'.

Each one of these words represents your highest values – the things that are important to you and bring a sense of meaning and richness to your life.

If all you did was achieve your goals without fulfilling your values, your success would be empty and chances are your life would feel hollow and you would feel empty on the inside. You might have money, but you certainly would *not* be rich.

When you imagine what you would like to have in your richer life, I want you to notice if it makes you feel really good to think about it. If it doesn't, you need to be more creative.

Think about it – if you rely solely on meeting your goals as a measuring stick for your success in life, you are going to spend an awful lot of time feeling like a failure. But when you focus on living your values each day, you are not only more likely to reach your goals, you are more likely to enjoy your life. It doesn't matter if you achieve every single one of your goals in exactly the time frame you laid out. As you live your values, your life becomes richer and richer.

So let's begin to explore both what you want to create in your life and what you want to create it for – your vision and your values ...

A LIFE OF VALUE

1. Imagine that it's five years from today and your life is filled with the most wonderful things imaginable. Your life is truly rich in every way!

   Write a paragraph or two about what has happened in each of the following areas:

   Health
   Career/finances
   Relationships
   Spirituality
   Lifestyle

2. Go back through each paragraph you have written and circle, underline or highlight each key goal or milestone that emerged.

3. Now, for each of the major goals or milestones you have identified, ask yourself: 'What do I want this for? What will having this give me?'

   Your answers should be just a few words long – things like 'a feeling of joy', 'a sense of achievement', 'freedom' or 'making a contribution'.

4. Repeat this exercise often over the next few weeks. You can play with different time frames (i.e. one year, ten years, etc.) and different categories (i.e. 'business success', 'leaving a legacy', 'family', etc.).

   Each time you do, different things will emerge. Over time, you will notice a core set of goals and values appear again and again – these are the ones that you will use to create your rich vision of the future in the exercises that follow.

Each time you run through this exercise, you are programming that genius computer inside your mind to begin creating what it is that you want in order to live a rich life. Now, we will begin to automate the process so that you can move towards your rich life every single day.

Time for a change

Simply by having taken the time to think through your goals and values, your life will begin to improve. But we are now going to use the power of your unconscious mind to take the whole game to another level.

All the rich thinkers I worked with in creating this book were firm believers in the power of intention – our ability to focus our minds on a vision of the future and unleash an unstoppable force within ourselves for its achievement! We are now going to begin the process of programming your mind to pursue what you want with greater intention than ever before.

The first step in doing this is to begin to become aware of your brain's own unique way of representing time.

Without thinking about it, point to the future. Do it now.

Next, point to the past. Again, no thinking – just point!

Now, notice the direction that time moves for you. Does the future extend out in front of you with the past behind you? Or is the past on the left and the future on the right?

There are no right or wrong answers – however your brain codes time is perfect for you. As you do the following exercise, you will become even more clear about your own internal 'timeline' ...

DISCOVERING YOUR TIMELINE

1. Think of something that you do each day, like cleaning your teeth or having your breakfast. When you picture yourself doing that tomorrow, is the image in front of you, to the right, or to the left? How far away is it? Point to it now ...

2. Next, think about doing the same activity next week. Is the picture further to the right or to the left? In front of you or behind you? Closer or further away? Once again, point to where you 'see' the image in your mind.
   What about last week? Where do you picture doing that same activity one week ago?

3. Now think about doing the same activity one month into the future: Is the picture closer or further away? More to the right or the left? In front or behind? Higher or lower?
   What about one month ago, in the past? Where do you picture having done that same activity then?

4. Finally, imagine yourself doing that same activity six months into the future. Where is that picture – closer or further? Left or right? Higher or lower?
   How about six months ago – point to that image now ...

5. Imagine that all these images are connected by a line – like doing a giant 'connect the dots' puzzle in your mind. This is your 'timeline' – the way your unconscious mind represents time.

When you have a sufficiently compelling future, all of your resources are automatically directed towards bringing that future about. And the really wonderful thing is that you will find yourself moving towards that future every single day.

For example, when I did this with a client recently, he made an image of himself sitting at dinner with his family and friends. They were all celebrating his latest success at work. There was an incredible sense of prosperity about them, like they never needed to worry about money again. They were planning their luxury holiday to the south of France and joking about how much fun they were going to have sipping champagne and soaking up the sun.

What he really enjoyed about the picture was that he seemed so grounded and happy in himself – there was a real sense of having 'arrived' both spiritually and materially.

In the same way, this next exercise will assist you in programming a compelling future into your unconscious mind. Used in conjunction with the hypnosis CD, it will supercharge all your efforts for success ...

CREATING YOUR RICH VISION NOW

1. Imagine it's a year in the future and you have had the richest year of your life.

   What has happened in your relationships, career, health, finances, spiritual life? What new thinking and behaviours have you practised? Who are you becoming?

   Which of your longer-term goals have you already achieved? Which ones are already well underway? Which ones have faded into the background?

   What is it like to live your values every single day? How have they changed and evolved? Which ones have become even more important? Which ones have faded away?

2. Now, create an ideal scene that represents all that you most want to happen in your positive future. Make sure you can see yourself in that future looking really positive and happy. It can be realistic or symbolic.

   Design your 'ideal scene' now. Where are you? Who are you with? What makes your life so much richer? What do you like about it most?

3. Take that image and put it on to your timeline one year into the future. Make sure the image is really big, bright, bold and colourful. You'll know you're doing it right because it feels really good just to imagine it.

4. Next, you are going to fill in the blanks between then and now.

   • Make a slightly smaller picture and place it a few months before the big picture of what needs to happen before that.

   • Make an even smaller picture and place it a few months before that picture of what needs to happen before that.

   • Make an even smaller picture and place it a few months before that picture of what will need to happen before.

   You should now have a succession of pictures connecting the present with your positive, compelling future. The images should get progressively bigger with better and better things happening in them.

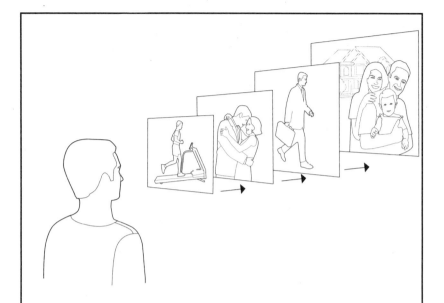

5. Look at those pictures and let your unconscious mind lock in the road map to your richer life over the next year.

6. Now, float up and out of your body and into each picture. Take a few moments to fully experience each step you will be taking on the path to greater success.

7. When you get to the big picture of your ideal scene, really allow yourself to enjoy experiencing it fully. What will it be like to have everything you want?

8. Finally, come back to the present and look out once again at your future timeline. You can feel confident in the knowledge that you have now created a map for your unconscious to use as a guide in bringing about the future you are longing to create!

You can repeat this exercise as often as you like. Each time you do, your future will become a little bit more real and your life will feel a little bit richer!

FREQUENTLY ASKED QUESTIONS ABOUT 'CREATING A RICH VISION'

Q. What if I can't visualize? I tried to find my timeline but I felt like I was just making it up!

One of the ways we make sense of the world is through the pictures we are continually making in our imagination. For example, if I ask you to think about your front door, you can remember what it looks like – what colour it is, the size, even what side the door handle is on. This is important, because otherwise you wouldn't be able to know where you live. You need to be able to visually imagine what things look like so you can recognize them when you see them in the real world.

These pictures in our mind have a powerful effect upon everything we do. The reason so many people believe they can't visualize is that they expect the pictures in their head to be as vivid and realistic as what they see on the outside. That would be disastrous! You have to have some way of knowing what's real and what's imagined.

As far as feeling like you were just making it up, that's fine. As long as you can do the exercise, you're doing the exercise perfectly. As you progress through the book and continue listening to the hypnosis CD, your ability to visualize will improve and your pictures will become clearer and clearer.

Q. I've read everything and done all the exercises, but I don't really feel like I know what to do in order to make money. What did I miss?

Part two of the book!

The second half of this system is packed with information, strategies and techniques for creating money and living a rich life. When you're ready to begin, just turn the page ...

PART TWO

Let's Go Make Money!

CHAPTER SEVEN

How to Make Money

HOW TO MAKE MONEY

> *The best way to come up with a really good idea is to come up with a lot of ideas.*
>
> LINUS PAULING,
> Nobel Prize-winning
> scientist

As I said in my book *Change Your Life in 7 Days*, if you want to create massive financial abundance, it is necessary to first recognize that your ability to make money is intimately linked to your ability to add, create and provide value, whether to a person, a project, a company or an enterprise. In fact, I'll say it even more clearly:

**Money is one of the rewards you get
for adding value to the lives of others.**

The more value you add to the world, the more money you will be rewarded with. But not all value is created equal. There are essentially three factors that affect your ability to make money from adding value:

- **Uniqueness** is whatever makes your product or service different from what's already out there. It's also about exclusivity – what your clients or customers can only get from you.

- **Scope** is the number of people you are able to impact with your offerings. Generally speaking, the more lives you add value to, the more money you will make.

- **Impact** refers to the amount of value you are adding to someone's world. Making a significant difference to someone's business, relationships and life will generally be rewarded at a higher rate than giving them a cup of coffee in the morning.

The more unique your offering, the more people it can reach, and the more it can impact them, the more money you will make. This is why a movie star can make more money than a teacher – while the impact of a teacher can be far greater on the thirty or so people he or she teaches each year, the movie star adds a unique value to millions and is rewarded accordingly.

That's not to say we need to engage in shallow pursuits to make more money. Mahatma Gandhi, known and revered throughout the world for his life of voluntary simplicity and his principled and peaceful role in creating independence for India, once said, 'It costs a lot of money to be my friend.' He knew that in order for the value he wanted to add to his countrymen to have scope and impact it would take millions. He simply chose to redirect those millions away from himself and towards the cause he believed in with all his heart.

A question of wealth

One thing that distinguishes the millionaires and billionaires I have met from the vast majority of people is that they are continually asking themselves what I call 'wealth-creating questions', and taking the time to answer them. An example of a wealth-creating question is this:

What unique product or service would I like to provide that will be of massive value to the world?

These kinds of questions make your brain sort for wealth creating information and put you in a more resourceful state. If you are not happy with the answers you are getting back, you can either change the question or keep asking until you are. Your brain will keep searching for you until a useful answer has been found. You might need to do this once or for several days before you get an answer that just clicks, that fires you up with enthusiasm.

Einstein wasn't a conventional scientist, he was a patent clerk. He was exposed to new ideas all day long. He came up with equations that changed the world because he was asking smarter questions than the best scientific minds of his day.

To make lots of money, you don't have to be academically smart – a quick look at the biographies of the *Times* 100 Rich List will confirm that. You just need to ask smart financial questions, and you need to keep asking them until you get the answer you need.

You may not get an answer straight away, which is why you keep asking. The human mind is infinitely creative – just think of all that exists in the world, all the art, science, technology, business, all created by the human mind. Stop for a moment and really think about these wealth-creating questions, and ask them over and over again:

- *How can I add value to the lives of others and most easily make money?*

- *What will people pay for that I can easily and happily provide them with?*

- *What are the ways can I most easily and enjoyably reach financial freedom?*

- *What would I love to create that people would love to give me money for?*

Spend the next few days asking yourself those questions over and over again until ideas just pop into your mind. The hypnosis CD that accompanies this book will further instruct your unconscious mind to go on a creative search for answers to the wealth questions.

Simple as it may seem, the exercise I am about to share with you is one of the most powerful in this entire book ...

THE MILLIONAIRE'S NOTEBOOK

1. Go out and get a special notebook or journal to use for this exercise – whatever makes you feel great about carrying it around with you and using it regularly. (Richard Branson told me that many of his best business ideas were written on the back of napkins or envelopes!)

2. Each day for the next 30 days, write down at least 10 answers to the wealth-creating questions above and any others you may think of. Your answers do not have to be practical, or, for the purposes of this exercise, legal – just let your creative mind flow.

3. At the end of the 30 days, you will have at least 300 ways to make more money by adding more value to the world!

Would you like to double your money, starting today?

One particular question I love to ask of anyone interested in making more money is this:

> When you have exhausted all possibilities, remember this – you haven't.
>
> THOMAS EDISON, inventor

If you woke up one morning in a place where you knew no one, with £100 in your pocket, how long would it take you to double your money and how would you do it?

While many people's first answer is 'I don't know' or 'I couldn't', when I ask them to really take the time to think about it, nearly everyone comes up with something.

Some people decide that they would look for something to buy that would be of interest to the local populace (umbrellas if it's rainy, suntan lotion if it's hot, etc.) and then sell it on at a profit.

Another guy said he would rent a camera and take pictures of people who looked like tourists and offer to sell them to them. He worked out that after just a few weeks he would be able to buy his own camera and develop his business.

Still others would offer a service – whatever it is they have a gift or skill for that if they needed to, could be easily translated into cash.

Let's begin exploring your hidden wealth (those ideas and resources that are already available to you but up until now you haven't thought of as 'money makers') with this same simple exercise …

DOUBLE YOUR MONEY

Let's do it now ...

1. If you woke up one morning in a place where you knew no one, with £100 in your pocket, how long would it take you to double your money, and how would you do it?

To help you in exploring this further, think through your answers to the following questions:

- What are you an expert at? What do you know (or would enjoy knowing) more about than most people?

- What are your skills and abilities? What do you do (or could you do) better than most people?

- What have you accomplished up to this point in your life that other people respect or admire you for?

- What things do you have that other people would love to have?

- What do you currently do for free that people will pay you for?

2. Once you've doubled your money, how long would it take you to double it again (i.e. from £200 to £400)? How would you do that?

The more often you do this exercise, the less dependent you will become on money as the source of your wealth.

When I asked this question of some of the rich thinkers, their answers were even more dramatic.

- Peter Jones said that he would find products he could buy and then sell them like a street trader. It wouldn't matter what the products were, because he'd be doing it to accumulate enough money to invest in other things he could be more passionate about and that would have uniqueness, and greater scope and impact.

- The young property magnate Nick Candy's answer was extremely bold. He said that he would find the richest entrepreneur in town and say to him: 'Invest £1 million in me and I will give you a 20 per cent return within a year.'

- Dame Anita Roddick's answer was equally fascinating. At first, she said that in order to get by she would simply offer her services as a nanny, or cook. When I asked her what she would do if the goal was to make millions, her rich-thinking business brain kicked into overdrive. She said, 'Elderly people don't use computers because they're too bloody complicated. So I would find somebody smarter than I am, a really smart computer programmer, and ask them to design a computer that works on only four buttons – on, off, files and internet. I would offer them an equal partnership in our new business. I would guarantee them that if they could design it, I would be able to sell it and make it into a great business.'

The point of the exercise is to demonstrate that we all have the capacity to create money using nothing but the ideas in our heads and the skills in our personal arsenal. This is one of the most important ideas you will learn on your path to riches:

You are your own money!

When you really realize this, you will never have to worry about 'not having enough in the bank to be safe'. Your true riches don't lie inside a bank, but rather live freely inside your mind.

Penis jokes and Irish dancing

One thing that will help you with the above exercise is to understand that you can make money from doing pretty much anything. I remember listening to Howard Stern when he had a group of Japanese visitors on his show. One of them asked him how much annual revenue his controversial radio show generated. Stern took the time to actually add up not only his salary and endorsements, but all the money the radio stations brought in through advertising and publicity because of his show. The total was in excess of one billion dollars.

There was silence on the air as the men clearly pondered the implications of that. Howard Stern then punctured the silence by saying, 'Who would have thought you could make over a billion dollars by telling penis jokes?'

Similarly, I recall a conversation with my friend Michael

Flatley, creator and star of *Lord of the Dance*, one of the biggest musical sensations of recent years: 'Who'd have thought that Irish dancing would make me hundreds of millions of pounds?'

Whether you think of such pop-culture sensations as beanie babies, cabbage patch dolls, pet rocks and sea monkeys or unplanned but wonderful inventions like marmalade, post-it notes and fax machines, the keys to wealth are most often found locked away in the files of our imaginations under the heading: 'Well, I'd love to but it would never work ...'

For example, two of the most successful products of the last 100 years, Coca-Cola and Levi's jeans, were both 'mistakes'.

Coca-Cola was originally a not very effective headache syrup developed by an enterprising pharmacist named John Pemberton. When he caught a couple of stock boys mixing his new syrup with water and drinking it in the back of his shop, he tasted it and realized that if he mixed it with soda water, it might be something that people would be willing to pay for.

As for 'blue jeans', they were developed when a would-be gold prospector named Levi Strauss travelled to San Francisco with merchandise he planned on selling to raise money to buy a stake in a mine. He failed to sell two large rolls of blue tent canvas. So he hired a local tailor to make overalls out of the tent fabric and brass rivets. The demand for his new, sturdy trousers was so great he never did go looking for gold.

When you realize that there are no limits to the number of different ways people make money, the question changes from 'Is there a way for me to make money?' to ' How would I like to make money?'

The 'real' value of what you have to offer

> *In life, you don't get what you deserve, you get what you negotiate.*
> CHESTER L. KARRASS, writer

Once you master the art of creating and adding value, you simply need to learn to exchange that value appropriately. This is another area where rich-thinkers do things just a little bit differently. Exchanging time for money is ultimately a limited game – no matter how you charge, there are only 24 billable hours in a day. But when you learn to charge for the value you are creating, there are no limits to how much you can earn.

For example, what do you think is a reasonable mark-up on a product or service? 10 per cent? 50 per cent? 100 per cent? Would you be able to justify a 4,000 per cent mark-up?

A friend of mine is a very successful salesman. I remember being astounded by a deal he once did where software that cost his company around £200,000 to research and develop and less than £50 to manufacture was sold for over £10,000,000.

When I asked him how he justified such an enormous difference between the cost and the price, he said, 'I knew from the research we had done that using our software would save the company nearly £50,000,000. After some negotiation, we settled on a payment of approximately 20 per cent of their benefit.'

The whole thing reminded me of one of my favourite stories:

In days gone by, there was a wealthy man who had a wonderful steamship, but as is the way with expensive things, it was prone to breaking down. Normally, the ship's engineers could get it going again, but one day, after a particularly difficult journey, the engine failed, and no one could get it going again.

One by one, every mechanic and engineer in the land was summoned to try to fix the engine, and one by one they failed. Finally, word came to the wealthy man of a wise old shipmaker who might be able to help, but at a hefty price. The wealthy man agreed at once.

Soon an old man who looked like he must have been fixing ships for a hundred years arrived. He carried a large bag of tools with him, and he immediately went to work. He inspected the large network of pipes leading to and from the engine very carefully, occasionally placing his hand upon the pipes to test for warmth.

Finally, the old man reached into his bag and pulled out a small hammer. He gently tapped against one of the pipes. Instantly, the sound of steam rushing through the pipes could be heard and the engine lurched into life as the old man carefully put his hammer away.

When the wealthy man asked the shipmaker what he owed him, the bill came to ten thousand pounds, a princely sum then.

'What?!' the ship-owner exclaimed. 'You hardly did anything at all! Justify your bill or I will have you thrown into jail.'

The old man began to scrawl something onto a ragged piece of paper he pulled from his pocket. The wealthy man smiled as he read it and apologized to the shipmaker for his rude behaviour.

This is what it said:

For tapping with a hammer £1
For knowing where to tap £9,999

VALUE-BASED PRICING

1. Think about a product or service you are currently involved in selling. (If you are an employee, you are the product; if you are not in business at all yet, think about the value you can provide doing what you want to do.)

   Example: A stabling service for horses.

2. Determine what you think is a 'fair' price based on how much effort you put in, how much it costs you to develop the product or service you offer, and 'fair market value'.

   Example: Between maintenance on the property, food for the horses and a reasonable hourly wage, it seems fair to charge £300 a month for stabling a horse.

3. Next, work out as best you can what the value of what you're offering is to the other party. If you come up with any unanswerable questions, write them down. By researching the answers to these questions, you will gather the critical information that allows you to set a price based on 'value to them' as opposed to 'cost to you'. When all else fails, try asking them!

   Example: Most people with horses are less concerned with cost than care. And some people will invest over £100,000 in their horse over the course of its lifetime. If I knew that my horse was not only safe but would receive proper exercise, training and grooming while it was stabled, £1,000 a month would be well worth it to me.

4. You now have two numbers to use in your negotiation. The 'value to them' number will give you a good idea of where to pitch your pricing; the 'cost to you' number will give you a clear bottom line, below which you would walk away from the deal.

Grow rich while you sleep

As you become more and more skilled at spotting opportunities to add value and exchange that value for money, you will begin to accumulate reserves of cash. If you use that 'extra' money wisely, you can create a lifetime of financial abundance without having to keep working harder, longer or even smarter.

When the Blackberry was first introduced, a friend of mine demonstrated how he could keep track of how much money he was making while sitting at dinner. Although he started his life working in a factory, he now travels the world and has made millions.

Another friend, who loved to cook, saved and saved until she had enough of a down payment to start a restaurant. For the first few years she worked there every day and loved it. Now, she's opened two more restaurants and only works a couple of days a week. Meanwhile, the restaurants have made her financially independent.

Another friend is a successful musician who has put his creative energy into writing music that brings joy to the world. One of his songs has become very successful – so successful that he refers to it as his 'pension'. Even when he is asleep, radio stations around the world are playing his song and making him money.

This is perhaps the ultimate 'secret' to making money:

Don't put yourself to work for money when you can put money to work for you!

The way you do this is by investing your time, energy and money in what are called 'profit-generating assets'.

What is a profit-generating asset?

Anything you own that makes you money whether or not you show up to work. This could be a rental property or a piece of intellectual property; a business, product or invention; an effective employee or even an effective brand.

This is also one of the fundamental differences between how rich thinkers and poor thinkers spend their money:

- Rich thinkers spend their money on assets – things that will make them more money in the future.
- Poor thinkers spend their money on expenses and liabilities – necessities that cost them money now and pointless things that seem fun at the time but will cost them more money in the future.

This is also the crucial difference between using a job to make money and using an asset – the asset will continue to make you money long after you've stopped working. And these days, with the internet continuing to shrink the global market, creating and/or investing in profit-generating assets is easier than ever.

CREATING A FINANCIAL SNAPSHOT

1. Make a list of any current or potential profit-generating assets you currently own. It's OK if you don't have many, but here are some of the commonly overlooked ones:

   Examples:
   My computer – I can use it to start an internet-based business.
   My home – I could rent out a room or create a home office.
   My telephone – I can use it to make sales calls and negotiate deals.

2. Now, make a list of your current liabilities.

   Examples:
   Car payments.
   Time share.
   Anything you own that is difficult and/or expensive to maintain.

3. Are your current spending patterns those of a 'rich thinker' or 'poor thinker'? Evaluate any money you spend from now on according to these criteria.

4. Brainstorm at least 20 ways to either increase your profit-generating asset column or decrease your liability column in the next month.

5. Take action on your best ideas!

Money-making mastery

If you aren't yet getting excited about doubling your money, creating profit-generating assets and starting your millionaire's notebook, chances are it's because at some level you don't yet believe you've got what it takes to really add massive value to the world and, in doing so, make a lot of money.

In fact, until you really begin to see yourself as someone capable of making a difference in the world around you, it will be difficult for you to make any real impact on your net worth.

The final exercise in this chapter (along with repeated listening to the hypnosis CD) will help you to accelerate the process ...

AN EXPERT AT MAKING MONEY

1. Think of something you already do well. It could be a hobby, a sport, or even something to do with your current job or occupation. When you imagine it, notice the location of the image you make. Where do you picture it – is it in front of you, to the left or right?

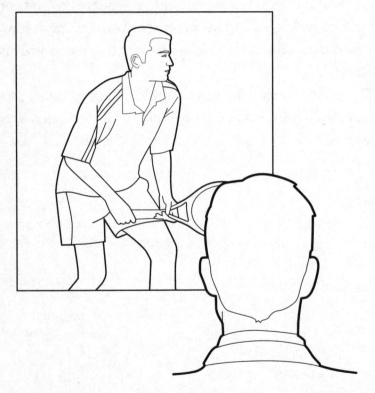

2. Next notice the size of the image – is it life size, larger than life, or smaller? Does it have much colour? Is it bright or dim?

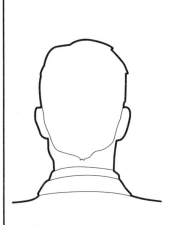

3. Now, stop for a moment and imagine what it would look like if you had the ability to make money easily. What do you imagine, and more importantly where is the image located? In front of you, to the left or right?

4. In a moment I'd like you to move the picture of you making money and put it exactly where the picture of you doing something extremely well was located. Make it the same size and brightness too.

    Some people like to just slide one image across to where the other was, other people like to imagine an elastic band on the back of the image of making money that is attached to the horizon, so the image shoots off and then snaps back into the position where the image of going something well was located.

However you choose to do it, do it now ...

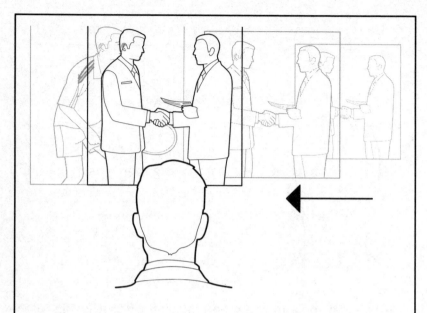

5. In the future, each time you think about making money, take a moment to make sure your new picture is firmly in place!

FREQUENTLY ASKED QUESTIONS ABOUT 'HOW TO MAKE MONEY'

Q. What if I couldn't think of any ways to double my money?

It's important to remember that making money is a skill – and so is applying your creative imagination. While some people are able to answer this question almost immediately, other people get caught up in trying to get the 'right' answer and consequently for a short time don't get any answer at all.

Go ahead and give yourself more time. When it comes to creativity, the harder you push yourself the harder it will be. Relax, don't censor yourself and let the answers flow.

Q. I own my own home and my own car. Aren't those assets?

Many people confuse an asset with a liability. An asset is anything you own that makes you money; a liability is anything you own that costs you money. While big houses, fancy cars, boats and aeroplanes may be some of the extremely enjoyable trappings of financial abundance, each one of them diminishes your bank balance over time. That same amount of money invested in a profit-generating asset will ultimately allow you to enjoy all of those same trappings at a fraction of the cost.

Of course, some liabilities are necessary. Only the most committed or foolhardy students of wealth will forge ahead without securing the basic necessities of hearth and home. Other liabilities will ultimately help you to generate assets – try progressing in today's marketplace without a phone or access to a computer and you may find yourself struggling.

Perhaps the most useful 'liability' you can spend your money on is your education – not just school, but the kinds of skills they don't teach in school, like how to start a business, negotiate a deal, add more value and make more money.

Q. It sounds like if you already have money this could work for you, but I'm in debt and barely make enough to make ends meet. How am I supposed to invest in profit-generating assets?

One of the biggest surprises to me when I first began study-ing rich thinkers is how little of their own money they use in creating their wealth. As with most investments, profit-generating assets don't have to be paid for all at once. This is the principle of leverage in action – using your expertise and other people's money to get involved in investments that are beyond your current means.

While some investments will require you to provide your own capital, in most cases you can get outside funding for some or all of the investment once you can demonstrate the soundness of your business plan. For example, if you want to buy a home that costs £300,000, the bank requires a survey to prove the house is a solid investment. Once the survey has shown the property is sound, they will put in the majority of the money to allow you to buy it.

In chapter ten, I will share with you a simple template you can use to begin assembling your plan, and in chapter eleven we'll discuss the key skills and strategies you can use to get potential investors to back you.

CHAPTER EIGHT

Assembling Your Wealth Team

ASSEMBLING YOUR WEALTH TEAM

> *I would rather have 1 per cent of a hundred men's efforts than 100 per cent of my own.*
>
> JOHN PAUL GETTY, oil billionaire

Many years ago, Henry Ford, founder of Ford Motors, was involved in a libel trial with a Chicago newspaper that had accused him of being 'ignorant'.

In an attempt to prove their case, the lawyers for the newspaper put Mr Ford on the stand and asked him a series of questions designed to 'prove' their assertion that he was ignorant.

The 'master mind' principle

After putting up with round after round of difficult questions, Ford tired of the game. He leaned forward and said to the lawyer:

If I should really want to answer any of the foolish questions you have just been asking me, I have a row of electric push-buttons on my desk. By pushing the right button, I can summon to my aid people who can answer any question I desire to ask concerning the business to which I am devoting most of my efforts.

Now, will you kindly tell me why I should clutter up my mind with general knowledge, for the purpose of being able to answer questions, when I have people around me who can supply any knowledge I require?

Needless to say, Ford won the case, and in so doing demonstrated the power of what bestselling wealth author Napoleon Hill calls 'the master mind principle' – the 'coordination of knowledge and effort ... between two or more people' that creates a powerful group mind that is far greater than the sum of its parts.

The surprising secret of rich thinkers

When people first create their visions, there is sometimes a sense of impossibility – even though they can see the result they are wanting to create, they can't imagine a path to getting there that doesn't involve struggle, sacrifice and pain.

The first thing I did after creating my first rich vision back in my early twenties was put it away in a desk drawer and pretend it never happened. It seemed ridiculous to me that an average kid from Enfield was going to be able to go out and succeed in the world when so many before had tried and seemingly failed. But that's because I didn't yet know about the secret weapon of rich thinkers. As my friend the success coach Michael Neill says:

**Every worthwhile accomplishment is the result
of a team effort!**

Every rich thinker I worked with in assembling this system told me some variation of this same idea – the master key to riches is knowing how to harness the collective efforts of a truly great team. I can't tell you what a relief it was for me to discover that I didn't have to do it all myself. I didn't have to know everything. What I needed to do was to get really good at choosing and motivating really good people.

In my life, I have not met one successful person who has done it all on their own. In fact, many of the people I have studied are proud of their ability to choose good people and manage the relationship with them. It is a prerequisite of success that you surround yourself with people who can help you to add value and manage your money.

Now when I say team, I don't mean you have to suddenly go and hire lots of people as your employees. I'm not even suggesting that everyone who supports a successful person thinks of themselves as part of that person's wealth team. Many of the people who have helped me most in my life have never met me, be they authors, speakers or role models I have learned from.

The point is, you can't do it yourself, and trying to carry all your goals on your own back will ultimately crush you. While I believe every one of us has every reason to be proud of whatever level of achievement we have currently attained, how far could we have got without the efforts of those who built the businesses that support us, created the products we use or earned the money that eventually finds its way into our bank accounts. Imagine how slow the pace of business would be if we had to make our own computer chips from silicon we harvested using simple tools made from wood and flint we found lying around the cave!

When you recognize that there's no such thing as DIY success, you can begin actively cultivating the ideal relationships to support you as you move forward towards creating your rich vision.

DRAFTING YOUR DREAM TEAM FOR WEALTH

1. Write down the description of the rich vision you created for yourself in chapter six – the goal in life, tangible or intangible, that for you would be the epitome of success and fulfilment.

   If you are having any trouble with this step, who do you know who could help you in uncovering what matters to you most?

2. Make a list of your strengths and weaknesses in relation to your big dream – those things you do extremely well and those things you do not, which interfere with your success.

   If you're not sure about your strengths and weaknesses, ask the people closest to you. You may be surprised at what you discover!

3. Next to each weakness, write down the characteristics of the ideal person to support you in this area.

   Examples:

   I'm terrible at bookkeeping – I want someone scrupulously honest, detail oriented and great at maths.

   I can't sell myself – I want someone who is naturally extroverted and a big believer in what I do.

   I'm disorganized – I want someone who likes structure and loves making lists and charts and diagrams.

4. Now, make a list of the people who are already part of your wealth team. This can include friends, family, neighbours and colleagues, but it can also include authors and role models who inspire and educate you, be it in person or through their books, tapes, videos, etc.

   Remember, your wealth team is made up of those people who support you in the pursuit of your dream and/or your day-to-day life, regardless of whether they think of themselves this way!

5. Next, make a list of all the roles you would like fulfilled if you were building your own wealth support team from scratch.

   Example: Coach, Mentor, Cheerleader/Motivator, Teacher/Trainer, Financial Adviser, Lawyer, Accountant, etc.

   Answer each of the following questions:

   - How many of these roles are or could be filled by members of your current 'team'?

   - If you were going to create your 'ideal wealth team', who would you most want to fill these roles?

   - Who on your current wealth team could help you find the 'missing' players on your ideal wealth team?

Refining your team

> *You can't do it all yourself. Don't be afraid to rely on others to help you accomplish your goals.*
>
> OPRAH WINFREY, billionaire talk-show host

I have noticed that many people take advice from others who are unqualified to give it. Your uncle Frank may be the nicest man in the world, but unless he is rich, why would you listen to what he says about money?

One of the most fascinating experiences I had when taking myself through the above exercise was making a list of the people who were already on my team simply by virtue of the fact that I sought advice from them.

Firstly, I was surprised how many people were on the list. Then I started to think about how they contributed. Some of the people I sought advice from had lots to say, although if I was honest they hadn't achieved much themselves. A couple of them had been successful at making money, but were even better at losing it once they had made it. A few of the most qualified people on my list were the ones I spoke to least often! So I began to change the make-up of my team, using the process below.

Take a moment now to do this for yourself...

PRIORITIZING EXCELLENCE

1. Make a list of everybody you currently talk to about business or money, either professionally or casually.

2. Who on this list has given you advice in the past that has made you money, or has supported you in reaching your goals?

3. Now prioritize the list by asking who has given you the advice that has made you the most money. Whose counsel has assisted you most in times of need?

4. Consider replacing or eliminating as many people from the bottom part of the list as you can.

5. Make sure the people on the top of your list feel valued. You can use any of the strategies from the section on 'Putting Your Team to Work' or create some of your own.

Expanding your wealth team

Assuming that you have by now identified some gaps in your current wealth team, the next step is to fill those gaps with the best people available to you.

In one of my favourite success books, *Simple Steps to Impossible Dreams*, author Steven Scott offers the following advice for recruiting mentors, which I have loosely adapted for recruiting members of your wealth team:

1. Your 'Dream Team'

Make a list of the people you would like to be on your wealth team. List the names in order of preference, starting with the potential members of your 'dream team'.

2. Research

For each person on your list, write down everything you know about them – likes, dislikes, interests and passions. Don't be afraid to ask around and do additional research – the better prepared you are, the better your meeting will go. Also, the more you know about their track record, the better choices you will make about who is on your team.

Nearly all the rich thinkers I modelled felt that track record was the number-one key to choosing an effective team member.

3. Prepare your approach

Use what you know and what you've learned from your research to decide whether to make your approach formal or informal, general or specific, overt or covert. While 'Hey – fancy being on my wealth team?' may work for some of the people on your list, it's liable to get you kicked out of as many rooms as it gets you into.

At the very least, you should be able to say exactly what it is you would like them to help you with, and why, in less than a minute.

Example: Ryan, I'm always amazed at how much smarter I am when I'm talking with you than the rest of the time. Would you be willing to let me bounce my business ideas off you before I approach the banks?

4. Make contact

The old rule about asking for help was: *In person is best, on the phone is second best, and a letter is a distant third.* These days, however, you may find e-mail gives you access to people you would never have been able to speak to in the past.

Whatever your means of communication, try to be brief – most people worth getting help from value their time!

Putting your team to work

> *When spider webs unite, they can tie up a lion.*
>
> ETHIOPIAN PROVERB

Now that you're in the process of building your wealth team, how do you get the most out of it?

Here's a short list of some of the most useful ways to get maximum value out of the people on your team.

1. Keep in touch

I like to keep a separate list in my address book and contact management software for members of my wealth team. I make a point of contacting everyone on my team regularly whether I 'need' to or not.

Acknowledging my appreciation of their presence in my life is important, especially when work commitments may mean I'm not particularly present in their lives from time to time.

Because I've kept in touch with everyone on my team, when I do need a bit of advice or a helping hand, a quick flick through my wealth team roster will remind me of just the right person to call or e-mail to help me get back on track.

2. Don't be afraid to pay them

I hired somebody a few months ago on a good salary even though there wasn't a job vacancy at the time and there certainly wasn't a big budget to employ this person. So what did he say that made me decide to back him?

He knew me and about my business and approached me to explain how he could develop an area of my business whose potential I had overlooked. The story he told me was that he would generate enough money to pay for himself many times over.

I ran the figures several times, checked with my advisors and his story held up, although what finally made me hire him was what he said: 'I will be a wealth generator for you, every day I will wake up and ask myself how can I make you money.'

This is an excellent example of perceived value. Rather than just asking for a job, he told me how much money he was going to create and based his salary request on that.

Those people who get paid the most have their wealth thermostat set high and their belief in and passion about what they offer the world is strong.

It's true that some relationships work best when information and favours are exchanged on the basis of friendship and mutual support. But as money becomes less and less of an issue for you, don't be afraid to pay for it when friendship alone is not enough, or when you don't want to be obligated to return the favour one day. Even when money is tight, getting the right piece of assistance from the right person is nearly always worth the price.

3. Stay on top of things without smothering them

When it comes to living the life of your dreams, one of the least effective pieces of time-management wisdom is the notion of 'delegation'. In theory, delegation is a sound idea: we should be constantly looking for activities that we can delegate to our assistants, colleagues, spouses, and children, freeing up our time for 'more important things'.

There are, however, several problems with this approach in practice. Delegation tends to lead to a sort of 'out of sight, out of mind' approach to whatever has been delegated, which in turn can cost us time and energy in teaching, managing and worrying about whether or not tasks we could easily do ourselves are being adequately done by others.

A good rule of thumb is this:

Delegate the task, not the responsibility.

Something all the rich thinkers I studied agreed on was that you must be getting regular updates on where your team members are with the various tasks and projects you've delegated. Think of these check-ins as like having a GPS system for your goals – it can be tremendously helpful, but it only helps if you take the time to look at it and are willing to adjust your course when necessary!

4. Enrol them in your rich vision

Some members of your team will be motivated by money, some by status and power, others by challenge. Still others will only be interested in working with you if the work feels meaningful or the work environment is an enjoyable one.

> *Flowers flourish when they're watered, and shrivel up when they're not. People are no different. The best leaders are the ones who look for the best in people.*
>
> RICHARD BRANSON,
> billionaire entrepreneur

But the one thing that will override any of these concerns is a sense of ownership. When people feel truly involved in and a part of your rich vision, they will work far harder to support you than they would for any of their personal reasons. And the more vivid and real you can make your vision, the more people will want to be a part of helping you to make it happen.

When you take the time to paint an inspiring image of what you're up to and invite people to be a part of the picture, those who choose to join you will follow you pretty much anywhere you need to go!

One final technique for expanding your team ...

> *My motto has always been that anybody can do it better than me.*
>
> PAUL ORFALEA,
> founder and chairman of Kinko's

Think about a problem you have been having to do with money. Now, if you could ask anyone in the world for advice, who would you choose? What advice do you think they would give you?

In my hypnosis seminars, I often do an exercise called Deep Trance Identification. In order to deep trance identify with someone, it is simply necessary for the participant to be very familiar with that person's work. Ideally they will have read numerous books about them, watched them on videotape and/or listened to recordings of them.

I then place them in a trance, and instruct their unconscious minds to 'become' the person, a bit like the way a method actor fully immerses themselves into a character. They begin to move their body the way that person moves it and speak the way they speak.

The results are always amazing and often very funny. In doing what seems at first like a simple impersonation, they become more confident, optimistic, creative or intelligent. It's as though by taking on the physiology and speech of the person, they gain access to the same quality of thoughts.

What I've learned over the years is that you don't need to go into a deep trance in order to get the benefits of this exercise. You can use a very basic version of this psychological technique to gain a new perspective or insight into any area you would like to explore. It involves 'stepping in' to the perspective of somebody who is skilled at the area you are exploring and then looking at your present situation 'through their eyes'.

Here is all you need to do:

STEPPING INTO WEALTH

1. Close your eyes and imagine that the person you would most like to ask for advice about whatever it is you are working on is standing in front of you.

2. In your imagination, float into their body and see and hear things the way they would see and hear them.

3. Focus on whatever it is you are working on and notice what insights you get.

4. From the perspective of your wealth advisor, ask yourself each of the following questions:

   • What should I do more of?

   • What should I do less of?

   • What should I start doing?

   • What should I stop doing?

5. Take action on your best insights as soon as you possibly can!

Don't worry if this feels a bit strange at first – the more you do it the easier and more natural it becomes.

FREQUENTLY ASKED QUESTIONS ABOUT 'ASSEMBLING YOUR WEALTH TEAM'

Q. I don't have anyone on my team. How do I get started?

Since you started reading this book and listening to the CD, you have expanded your wealth team to include me and all the people I interviewed and modelled in assembling my system. You don't have to ring up Richard Branson, Philip Green or Anita Roddick for advice – their strategies for wealth and success are not only contained throughout this book, they are available in small doses in every interview they've done and every book they've written or contributed to.

Don't be afraid to 'call on us' anytime you need to, simply by thinking of a problem you'd like to solve and then thinking about the person you'd most like to help solve it!

In addition, anyone who helps you in any area of your life is on your team if you choose to think of them that way, from the barista who makes your coffee in the morning to help jumpstart your brain to the programmers at Google who are continually working to get you whatever information you need in a matter of seconds.

Once you recognize how much support you already have in your life, it will be much easier to begin putting together your 'dream team' as described earlier in this chapter.

Q. I'm having a hard time figuring out why anyone would want to be a part of my team – I don't have anything to offer them!

A friend of mine dates more beautiful women than anyone I know. As he's not particularly handsome or wealthy, I wanted to know his secret. Was it a great chat-up line? Was it the way he 'dressed to impress'? No. What set him apart was the number of women he was willing to ask.

Many high achievers get a tremendous amount of satisfaction and meaning in their lives by being of service to others. The key is to a) be willing to ask and b) not take it personally or blame them if they say no. If you are respectful of their time and genuinely enthusiastic about receiving assistance, you'll be pleasantly surprised at how often people are willing to help you on your way.

CHAPTER NINE

A Proven Formula for Success

A PROVEN FORMULA FOR SUCCESS

I find out what the world needs and then I proceed to invent it.

THOMAS EDISON, inventor

One of the most amazing discoveries I had when studying the high achievers for this book was that, while they all have their individual styles in business, they all share the same fundamental strategy for creating wealth. Broadly speaking, that strategy involves thinking about a product, service or business in an entrepreneurial way. In this chapter, I will show you how you can use this same wealth-creating template to create your own successful projects.

I used to find the idea of 'entrepreneurship' a bit daunting, but then I spoke with Peter Jones, widely acknowledged as one of Britain's most successful young entrepreneurs. Despite his modest beginnings, his businesses have an annual turnover of £200 million. He pointed out to me that the word 'entrepreneur' simply means 'someone who gets paid for adding value'. When you are willing to think of yourself as a value creator, your 'job' becomes quite simple:

Identify a field where you would like to add value, then identify the value you would like to add.

Over the rest of this chapter, I will outline the six steps to wealth that emerged again and again as I studied the business geniuses for this book. I will then share a case study

– Richard Branson's development of Virgin Atlantic Airlines. Finally, you will get the chance to begin your entrepreneurial apprenticeship by choosing a product, service or business to get you started.

Do not worry if you are already in business or are determined to remain an employee – these same six steps will be of great use to you to find the hidden wealth in your current working situation, whatever it may be.

Let's get things started …

Step 1: Choose something you have a passion for or genuine interest in

> *You've got to be a believer in what you do.*
>
> SIR PHILIP GREEN, retail billionaire

Sol Kurzner is a billionaire hotelier with a business empire that spans the world. He told me that one of the secrets of his success was his genuine passion for hotels.

'You've got to totally love what you do,' he said, 'because you are going to be spending a lot of time doing it. And when things aren't necessarily going as well as you hoped, it is your enthusiasm for the business that will keep you going.'

Richard Branson began in magazines and then rock music; Peter Jones took his fascination with tennis and computers and used them first to set up a tennis academy and then a business selling computer accessories. In his words, 'Having a passion for what you do is very important, especially when you are going to be working all hours to try and make the business work. In addition, your passion and belief will motivate others around you.'

Of course, your passion and interest can come from what you hate as much as what you love. When Dame Anita Roddick started the Body Shop, she was as determined to provide a safe and animal-friendly alternative to the standard operating practices of the cosmetics industry as she was to create a vehicle for putting her beliefs into action about what truly mattered in the world.

Step 2: Figure out where you can add value

Once you have identified something you have a genuine interest in and passion for, you then need to look for what you can bring to that field that isn't already there.

> *Entrepreneurs are visionaries – they see things other people don't see.*
>
> DAME ANITA RODDICK, founder of the Body Shop

Here are some of the questions the rich-thinking entrepreneurs ask themselves in examining the potential to add value to any business, product or service:

- Who is already making money in this area?
- What sets apart the most successful people in this field from the rest?
- What's missing? What isn't being done?
- What do the people who are already using this product or service *really* want?
- What can I offer that's different to everyone else?

Stelios Haji-Ioannou, founder of EasyJet and more than a dozen related businesses, summed up the essence of step 2 when he said: 'People are grateful when you make a difference in their lives. That is the essence of any successful business.'

Step 3: Vividly imagine every detail of how the business will work

One of the surprising differences between the most successful entrepreneurs I interviewed and the rest was their willingness to take the time to vividly imagine the details of every new enterprise before leaping into action.

For example, Sol Kurzner designs a hotel in his mind long before he builds them in the real world. He imagines every detail – how it will look, how each surface will feel, how the whole environment will be. Richard Branson makes pages and pages of detailed notes, describing every aspect of the business in great detail.

Peter Jones actually 'interrogates' the whole concept, searching for both the obvious and hidden areas of potential profits and potential obstacles to its success. If the obstacles can be overcome and he can see the business working, he gets a massive burst of motivation. He vividly imagines the business working and keeps this visualization regularly in mind. He says, 'I am a great believer that it is always easier to achieve something that you have already done, even though I may have only achieved it in my own mind. This gives me great confidence.'

However you choose to do it, taking the time to build your business in your mind and/or on paper is an essential step in the process. Be sure to look at the downside as well as the up – the more potential obstacles you can foresee and solve in advance, the fewer real obstacles you will face and the easier it will be to overcome them.

Step 4: Evaluate the risks and decide which ones are worth taking

Retail billionaire Sir Philip Green told me how he once bought 2,000 shops without even going to see them. When I asked him how he found the confidence to do something so seemingly risky, he surprised me by saying, 'I

> *Whenever you see a successful business, someone once made a courageous decision.*
>
> PETER DRUCKER,
> writer

don't do risk. I do what I call "educated risk". In that instance, I didn't need to see the shops. I had downsided the deal and knew it was worth it. Essentially, I did my homework and then bet on my own judgement.'

Dame Anita Roddick went a step further and said she had never met a single entrepreneur who took risks. 'We all take calculated risks – in other words, we evaluate the upside and downside of any major decision and act accordingly.'

This willingness to take risks after calculating the upside and downside is a common one. The genius filmmaker George Lucas made billions from the merchandizing rights to his 'Star Wars' movies. When I spoke with him, he told me that he got the idea when he took a careful look at the potential upside and downside of the very first movie in the series.

'Everyone has since thought this was a clever financial strategy,' said Lucas, 'but the truth is that I was concerned that the film might not work commercially. I knew it had the potential to achieve "cult status", so I figured if I could make money on the merchandizing it would help me to fund another film.'

Here's a quick way to calculate the risk/reward ratio of any new enterprise for yourself ...

CALCULATING RISKS

1. Think about a decision you are considering making that feels a bit risky.

2. On a scale from 1 to 10, how much good could come of taking this risk if you are successful?

3. On a scale from 1 to 10, how much of a negative impact would this risk not working have on your business or in your life?

4. If the first number is bigger than the second, the risk/reward ratio is weighted towards action; if the second number is bigger than the first, it's probably best to find another way to proceed!

Step 5: Take Massive Action!

Another thing I noticed about the rich thinkers and successful entrepreneurs was that there is virtually no gap between their decisions and their actions. Once they decided to go ahead with a project, the first action steps were generally taken within 24 hours.

When Mark Burnett arrived in LA in 1982, he had $600 in his pocket and no return ticket. His first job was selling T-shirts on Venice beach. Today he is the most successful TV producer in the world. He told me his motto is 'jump in' – take action even if you are not entirely ready. He firmly believes that a major part of his success has been his willingness to go for what he's passionate about, even if he isn't completely convinced he can actually pull it off.

For myself, I like to think of action as the great equalizer. No matter what your level of intelligence, education or capital, a willingness to take massive action instantly puts you on an equal footing with the wealthiest men and women in the world.

Step 6: Expect obstacles, learn from setbacks and keep moving towards your goals

> *Whenever I have faced a setback I have dusted myself down and got on with the rest of my life because I believed in myself.*
>
> SIR PHILIP GREEN, retail billionaire

Although only some of the rich thinkers I worked with would describe themselves as optimists, all of them are realists. Nothing in life unfolds exactly as planned, and a road without bumps is almost certainly not headed anywhere worthwhile.

Rather than take obstacles as a reason to give up or a 'sign from the universe', the truly successful entrepreneurs simply use each obstacle as an opportunity for creative problem-solving and creative action. If a business ultimately doesn't work out, they pick themselves up, dust themselves off and move on.

This resilience comes from self-belief and thorough downside planning. Peter Jones shared his version of this process:

> *If obstacles keep occurring, I stop and ask: What can I learn from this obstacle? What do we need to do differently to make it work? I then create a new visualization of how the business needs to function and keep running this scenario in my mind until I know it will work. If another obstacle or challenge occurs further down the line, I can then return to my vision for guidance and motivation. While things may not always happen totally as I planned, I always get to my goal in the end.*

The success formula in action

When I asked Sir Richard Branson how he came to start Virgin Atlantic, he gave me a perfect example of the success formula as it works in the real world. In his words:

'I started an airline because I was flying all over the world to visit record companies – and the experience of flying on other people's airlines was dire. I thought that I could do it better. At that time, there was no in-flight entertainment, I was lucky to have a bit of something that looked like chicken dumped into my lap by a stewardess who wasn't smiling, the seats were uncomfortable, and flying was just a ghastly experience.' (*Step one*)

So he began to ask himself what was missing from the experience – what kind of an airline he would ideally like to fly on. He thought, 'You know, I'd quite like a massage. I'd quite like not to be stuck in my seat the whole flight – to go to a bar. I'd really like to have a choice of entertainment rather than just one film.' (*Step two*)

From that simple beginning – from those few rich thoughts – one of the largest and most successful airlines in the world was born. But before he took a single action, he imagined how the business would work in great detail. As he said, 'I'm a great believer in writing everything down – making long lists of things that need to be done. For the airline I wrote down pages of ideas. Basically, I love creating things. Creating a business is a bit like creating a painting. It might sound a bit big headed, but you're trying to create a work of art.' (*Step three*)

As soon as Branson had written his plan for Virgin Atlantic, he began looking for the risks. 'You have to protect yourself against the downsides,' he told me. 'So, because I knew nothing about the airline business, I decided that if after the first year people didn't like the experience they got on my airplanes, I wasn't going to risk the whole of Virgin group to keep things going. I find that when protecting against the worst eventuality, it's always worth trying to do as much as possible.' (*Step four*)

Once he'd finished writing his plan and calculated his downside, Branson took action. 'I set about trying to see whether it was actually possible to put all those ideas I'd had into practice,' he said. 'I remember just picking up the phone and ringing Boeing and asking: "Do you have a second-hand 747?" That's really where it all began.' (*Step five*)

When it comes to resilience, Sir Richard Branson is a true role model. 'As long as I've done everything I can to avoid something going wrong, I won't feel badly about it if it does. If a venture doesn't succeed, I'm good at just moving on. That's the lesson learnt, putting it behind me, and I think that it is important to be able to do that. It is important to be positive, learn from mistakes and learn from when things go wrong. I just pick myself up and move forward.' (*Step six*)

Choosing your vehicle for wealth

Having now been exposed to this proven formula for success, it is time for you to identify your own unique vehicle for wealth – a specific service, product or industry that you are going to add value to and use to begin bringing more money into your life than ever before. If you are already in a

> *The most difficult part of any business is getting started. It takes far more effort to make your first million than your second.*
> RICHARD DESMOND, billionaire publisher

business you love, use these steps to clarify what you're doing. If you're an employee, you can either use them to begin creating a business in your spare time, or to evaluate your current job's potential to bring you more money than you are making now.

Here are the three things that are crucial in choosing what you will do next to begin making more money:

1. Genuine interest

Remember, passion is important in any business, but your passion does not have to be directly connected to the business you are in. A genuine interest in that business, however, is essential. One of my friends has made a fortune in three very different businesses: oil, entertainment and sewage. While he wouldn't describe himself as passionate about all of them in the same way, he is genuinely interested in each one. What he is absolutely passionate about is the art and science of running successful businesses.

For me, I find that by marrying my passion for helping people to be happier with the kinds of things I am genuinely interested in, I am able to make money consistently in a wide variety of endeavours.

2. Ease of start-up

While there is a nearly infinite number of ways to make money, it matters far less what you could do than what you will do. And since the hardest part of any new venture is getting started, it only makes sense to choose something it will be easy to get started with.

So to get started, choose a product, service or business you could get up and running within one month. That means you need to pick something you already have sufficient understanding of, so that the learning curve will not be too steep. As you develop your confidence in your growing ability to make money, you will be able to take on projects with a longer and longer gap between getting started and getting rich.

3. Scalability

As we've discussed, there are two basic ways to make money. The first is to trade your time; the second is to leverage your resources. While the old adage is 'you'll never get rich working for someone else', the reality is you'll never get really rich trading your time for money. There are only 24 hours in a day, and even if you were to spend all of them working it would still be a limited-sum game.

A scalable business is one where you can make more money without working more hours, either by replicating your efforts (i.e. franchises, employees, etc.) or by charging for the value you create as opposed to the time you put in.

The next exercise is one of the most exciting you will do over the course of this book. By the time you are done, you will have chosen and/or refined your next vehicle for wealth!

You can do this exercise on your own, but be sure to take some time to review your answers with the appropriate members of your wealth team ...

CHOOSING YOUR VEHICLE

1. Make a list of everything you have ever been paid to do. Don't censor the list yet – you may be surprised at what you discover.

   Examples:
   Babysitting
   Sales
   Waitressing
   Investing
   Writing

2. Now, add anything to your list that you have thought about doing and/or always wanted to do.

   Examples:
   Writing books
   Hospice care worker
   Stunt pilot
   Property investor

3. Next, cross anything off the list you wouldn't be genuinely interested in spending at least the next year of your life focused on. (This is different from 'what you would most love to do' – it's just a way of ensuring that you are setting yourself up to win!)

4. Of the items remaining on your list, put a checkmark next to any that it would be easy for you to get started on within the next month.

5. Finally, put a checkmark next to the most easily scalable ideas – i.e. the ones you will be able to get far more out of than you could possibly put in. (If you're not sure how you would do that, ask someone from your wealth team to help you with this one.)

For most people, it is now readily apparent which of the things on the list will make the best vehicle to get started with. If you're still not sure, pick your top 2 or 3 ideas and do some additional research until the best choice becomes obvious to you.

Take your time with this exercise. When you find yourself getting so excited about your idea that you can't wait to move forward, you'll be ready to take the next step ...

FREQUENTLY ASKED QUESTIONS ABOUT 'A PROVEN FORMULA FOR SUCCESS'

Q. I'm overwhelmed! It seems to me there are a million things I could do. How do I choose just one?

One of the common reasons people have trouble choosing is they are scared of making a mistake. But this is backwards thinking. It is only by making mistakes that you can learn, and it is only by learning that you will succeed. The trick is to continually evaluate the potential downside so you are never moving forward without a plan for what you will do if it doesn't work out.

However, if it really does feel like there are a million things you could do, celebrate. This next idea can simply be the first of many.

Here are some additional questions to help you decide:

- What would you like to make money doing?
- Which of the items on your list do you feel most passionate about?
- What are the one, two or three ideas that give you the best and strongest feeling?

Q. How can I employ this formula if I want to stay as an employee?

There are two keys to making more money as an employee. The first is to continually look for ways to make yourself more valuable to your company. You can do this by generating more income and/or finding ways to save the company time and money.

The second skill is to make sure your company notices. Let them know what you've done, what difference it made and ask for what you want. This is what one popular business book calls 'the art of tooting your own horn without blowing it'.

If your company is aware of what you are doing for them but remain unwilling to reward you appropriately, it may well be time to move on. You may be surprised to discover how much your worth in the marketplace has grown.

CHAPTER TEN

The Simplest
Business Plan in
the World

THE SIMPLEST BUSINESS PLAN IN THE WORLD

> *Measure twice – cut once.*
>
> OLD PROVERB

All creative artists begin by making models of their work in some form before creating them in the world. Painters make sketches; architects make computer-generated or cardboard models of their buildings. Film directors create storyboards outlining every aspect of their movies, shot by shot, and some of the greatest songs in history began life as a set of lyrics scribbled on a napkin, beer mat or scrap of paper.

These models and mock-ups allow the artist to see their vision more clearly before they expend the effort to bring their vision to life. It makes it easier for them to notice what's already there and, more importantly, what's still missing.

Yet when I first talk to people about business plans, they generally roll their eyes and roll up their sleeves as though I'm asking them to dig a latrine in the middle of a swamp. But a business plan is not hard work and is not written in stone – it is a blueprint for a successful company, designed to be constantly adapted as things change and new information becomes available.

In fact, creating a business plan is not so much about what you write, but rather about how your thinking evolves in the process of writing it down. The changes a clear plan makes in your thinking and ultimately your destiny can be dramatic and profound. Through the process of vividly imagining every detail of what it will be like when your business is thriving, your mind stretches far beyond its usual limitations and your sense of possibility expands.

Some people even believe that something magical happens when you make a business plan and commit to its execution. Even before you take a single action, events often start to turn in your favour as the natural result of your commitment.

In the words of the Scottish Himalayan explorer W. H. Murray:

> *Until one is committed, there is hesitancy, the chance to draw back, always ineffectiveness. Concerning all acts of initiative and creation there is one elementary truth, the ignorance of which kills countless ideas and splendid plans: that the moment one definitely commits oneself, then Providence moves too.*
>
> *All sorts of things occur to help one that would never otherwise have occurred. A whole stream of events issue from the decision, raising in one's favour all manner of unforeseen incidents and meetings and material assistance which no man could have dreamed would have come his way.*
>
> *I have learned a deep respect for one of Goethe's couplets:*
>
> > *'Whatever you can do or dream you can, begin it.*
> > *Boldness has genius, power and magic in it.'*

Creating a plan for your business can bring out the best and worst in you. At times it will bring your positivity, enthusiasm and talents for creative thinking and problem-solving to the fore. At other times it might produce fear, procrastination and, when done in a team, strong differences of opinion. But it's a magnificent process, and in my experience one that is always ultimately beneficial.

I would go so far as to say that developing a plan and then putting that plan into action is often the only difference between a 'good idea' and a life-changing journey.

Creating your plan

In order to create a simple yet powerful plan for your own product or service, it will be helpful for you to make use of the questions that follow.

> *Failing to plan is planning to fail.*
> ROBERT SCHULLER,

The questions are divided into five major categories:

I. Purpose, Values and Vision
II. Current Reality
III. One-Year Outcomes
IV. Strategies
V. Action Plan

By the time you are finished answering these questions, you will be ready to create a simple business plan for your own venture. I have provided you with a template for creating your plan at the end of this chapter, along with an example of the current plan for my own training company.

If your business is already up and running, these questions will help clarify why you are in business and what you need to do to become and/or remain profitable. If you're starting a new venture, your answers will lay the foundations for both present and future success.

Do not underestimate the power of the questions in this book. They are simple by design.

When you know exactly what it is you are wanting to create, what other people are doing in the marketplace, what obstacles you may face, the resources you will tap into to overcome those obstacles and the relevant financial numbers, you and your business will be exponentially more prepared for what awaits you in the real world.

Not all of the questions you are about to read will be directly relevant to where you are right now, but the more of them you can answer, the more likely you are to succeed …

I. Purpose, Values and Vision

What does my business do? Explain your business idea in
500 words or less. _____

_____

_____

_____

_____

_____

_____

_____

How does it operate? _____

_____

_____

_____

Explain your business to a five-year-old child. _____

_____

_____

_____

Who are your customers? _____

_____

_____

_____

_____

What is the ultimate goal of this business? _____

_____

_____

_____

_____

_____

What would truly outrageous success look, sound and feel like? _____

_____

_____

_____

_____

_____

Why are you in this business? _____

_____

_____

_____

_____

How will you know when you are finished with this business? _____

_____

_____

_____

_____

_____

_____

_____

Here are 28 additional questions I have learned from working with rich-thinking business people, which you may find useful in clarifying your purpose, values and vision:

• What would you like to celebrate this time next year?

• What has made your business successful to date?

• What will make it successful over time?

• What will your company be known for?

• What is your role and how will you spend your time?

• Are you a local, regional or international company?

• Where are your customers?

• Who are your customers?

• Who can you partner with?

• Who are your advisors?

• When will this business be operational?

• Where will you be located?

• Why are you creating this business?

• Why will your customers buy your products or services?

• How will your business be financed?

• Why will people invest in your business?

• How does the business define success?

- How do you want to interact with your employees, suppliers and customers?

- Describe the most important characteristics of your product or service.

- Describe what your product or service won't/doesn't do.

- Describe the characteristics of your BEST customers.

- Describe the characteristics of the people you would be better off not serving.

- Describe the characteristics of successful businesses you admire and would like to emulate.

- Describe the characteristics of business you would NOT like to emulate.

- What are my core values? Which of these are most relevant to my business?

- What are my key strengths? Which of these are most relevant to my business?

- If everything goes well, what will your business look like in five years' time?

- If everything goes well, what will your life look like in five years' time?

II. Current Reality

As important as clarity of purpose, values and vision are to your success, an awareness of what's really going on in your business *right now* is even more important.

When you go through these questions, be sure to avoid the temptation to make things better or worse than they really are ...

In relation to my vision, here's what's currently going on:

_____

_____

_____

_____

What I have done up to this point to get things going:

_____

_____

_____

_____

_____

Our competitors include: _____

_____

_____

_____

_____

Is this business financially viable in its current form? Why? Why not? _____

_____

_____

_____

_____

_____

If not, how long will it be before we begin to make money? (Remember, base your answer on facts, not hopes or fears.)

_____

_____

_____

_____

What's our 'burn rate' (monthly expenditure)? How long can we stay in business at our current burn rate before we run out of capital? _____

_____

_____

_____

_____

Which of our employees generate more income than they cost? _____

_____

_____

_____

_____

III. Outcomes

An outcome is to your vision what a road sign is to a motorway – these are the markers and milestones that let you know how your journey is progressing …

At the end of the year, how will you define 'success' in relation to your business? _____

_____

_____

_____

Imagine that it is one year from today and it has been your best year yet … What have you achieved? What is your new 'current reality'? _____

_____

_____

_____

_____

_____

What are some of the longer-term outcomes for your business? _____

_____

_____

_____

_____

What are the medium-term outcomes?_____

_____

_____

_____

_____

_____

What are the one-year outcomes? _____

_____

_____

_____

_____

_____

IV. Strategies

Your strategies are the big-picture ideas about how you will achieve your one-year outcomes and fulfil your vision for success. As you play with these questions, you will find the level of specificity and detail that's perfect for you and your company ...

How will we achieve our outcomes for the year? _____

_____

_____

_____

_____

_____

To drive the business forward, I personally intend to:

_____

_____

_____

_____

_____

What are our major obstacles and how will we overcome them? _____

_____

_____

_____

_____

_____

_____

What is the competition doing?

_____

_____

_____

_____

_____

What's missing? Where can we add more value?

_____

_____

_____

_____

How will/do we reach our target audience (through what mediums/methods?

_____

_____

_____

_____

_____

Why will/do customers buy what we're selling?

_____

_____

_____

_____

We will market to our ideal customers by ... _____

_____

_____

_____

_____

I will make use of my wealth team to assist me with ...

_____

_____

_____

_____

_____

_____

_____

V. Actions

Here are the questions I have learned to use to generate the most useful actions I can take for my business on an ongoing basis.

What actions are currently on your to-do list? Of those actions, what are the 20 per cent that will make 80 per cent of the difference? (See the Pareto Principle on page 276.)

_____

_____

_____

_____

What have you been procrastinating about/not prioritizing that will make a significant difference to your business?

_____

_____

_____

_____

If you had all the staff you needed, what actions would you get them to take on your behalf?

_____

_____

_____

_____

Make a list of at least 100 actions you could take in the next 90 days to move your business forward. That's only a little more than one action a day:

Key outcomes:
My 100 actions

	action	✔		action	✔		action	✔		action	✔
1			13			25			37		
2			14			26			38		
3			15			27			39		
4			16			28			40		
5			17			29			41		
6			18			30			42		
7			19			31			43		
8			20			32			44		
9			21			33			45		
10			22			34			46		
11			23			35			47		
12			24			36			48		

	action	✔		action	✔		action	✔		action	✔
49			62			75			88		
50			63			76			89		
51			64			77			90		
52			65			78			91		
53			66			79			92		
54			67			80			93		
55			68			81			94		
56			69			82			95		
57			70			83			96		
58			71			84			97		
59			72			85			98		
60			73			86			99		
61			74			87			100		

Now, fill in the business plan form on the following pages. If you would like a full-size copy, send a blank e-mail to: simplestbizplan@paulmckenna.com

Company Name: _____

Purpose:
Why are you in business? What is the value you wish to add
to the world? _____

_____

_____

_____

_____

Values:
What are your core values? What do you want your business
to stand for? What are the principles you want your business
to stand on? _____

_____

_____

_____

Vision:
Paint a verbal picture of where your business will be when
it's fully grown. Inspire yourself! _____

_____

_____

_____

_____

Current Reality:
Where are you now in relation to your vision, physically and financially? Remember to stick to the facts and update this section regularly. _____

_____

_____

_____

Key Outcomes:
Where do you want your business to be in one year's time? In three years? Five years? What are the most important outcomes you are working towards right now? _____

_____

_____

_____

Core Strategies:
How will you get there? You don't need to get too specific here – broad brushstrokes are fine! _____

_____

_____

_____

Action Plan for the next ____ days:
What's next? And then? And then? _____

_____

_____

A business plan in action

On the following two pages, you can see an example of the current business plan for my training company. We update it at least once every three months to take into account any changes in our personnel, goals and the results we are producing in the world.

The only things that never change are our purpose and values – these are the cornerstones on which the company is built. The vision is a bit bigger than it was when I started back in 1993, but hasn't changed significantly for a while now.

It is important to recognize that this is not the only way to do this, nor am I suggesting that our values are the best values to have. Answering the questions in this chapter and creating this kind of plan is simply the most user-friendly way I personally have found to keep track of what's most important in my business and making sure that our actions are always aligned with our purpose, values and vision.

Company Name: McKenna.com

Purpose

To help people improve their lives using powerful, easy strategic change while making money and having fun. Providing excellent value to the end user.

Values

Excellence, honesty, ambition, integrity, informed decision-making, fun, entertainment, excitement, creativity, change, people-focus, communication, service, value, and paying good rates for great people.

Vision

We are a widely respected and well-known international organization, serving millions of people with the most powerful and up-to-date life-changing and life-enhancing techniques. We are a global brand for self-improvement with a specific focus on weight-loss, becoming rich (in every sense), confidence, and simple, powerful behavioural change. We provide this through TV shows, mail-order and downloadable products, and other forms of intellectual property for entertainment and educational purposes. We have created an active, interactive online community of millions of people around the world.

Every day, we help people to become more positive and create long-lasting changes in themselves and in the world. We do this quicker, more easily and more dramatically than anyone has done it before.

Current Reality

We have a stable, solid business regularly performing well and bringing in consistent profits with good cash position. We have the website up and running, 250,000 people on our database, with all technical resources in hand. We have a solid operational platform: good people, strong policies, a business plan with regular forecasting and management reviews, a motivated team who know their goals and the company's goals, and a strong plan of investment and developmental projects.

Current Challenges

Communicating the value of joining our online community. Finding ways to use the latest technology to most easily impart the best information and techniques to people through the internet. Continuing to increase the effectiveness of our techniques. Reaching a wider audience with what we do (breaking into emerging markets).

Key Outcomes

This year we will:

1. Make a financial return on the investments of the last few months: increased sales and reduction of indirect costs – so increased profit-ability.

2. Development into new territories (USA and other parts of Europe).

3. Database grows to 500,000+ people.

4. The community grows to the point where it is largely self-sustaining.

5. We are one of the largest online self-improvement organizations in the world.

Core Strategies

1. Implement a three-year strategy rotation:

Year 1 – Create massive awareness of the site through television shows and magazine articles. Create ongoing content and put in place systems for easy sustainability and focus on profit generation.

Year 2 – Initiate a re-investment programme in the business to support the expanding infrastructure: people, procedures, IT, cash.

Year 3 – Reap the solid profit return from year 1 and soft return from the year 2 investment programme. Continue to build a bigger and better team to support and underpin the new business requirements and increase in work.

Action plan for the next month

1. Meeting with key players to discuss current specifics.

2. Generate content and structure for site.

3. Decide what content is free and what is premium.

4. Email database with new offers.

FREQUENTLY ASKED QUESTIONS ABOUT 'THE SIMPLEST BUSINESS PLAN IN THE WORLD'

Q. I already have a business plan. Can I just skip ahead?

You could, but you'd be missing out. Even if you've got a business plan that really works for you, any additional information you discover through answering the questions in this chapter will increase your clarity about what it is you are doing and how you are going about doing it. And when it comes to overcoming obstacles and increasing profitability, clarity is power!

Q. I don't really want to start a business – I just want to make more money at my current job. How are all these questions relevant to me?

You will be surprised at how much you learn if you answer the questions as if the business you are working for is *your* business. You will begin to see opportunities for you to add value within your current company, which in turn will give you the leverage you need to expand or upgrade your current position and receive more money in return.

Q. Do I need to complete my business plan before I read the rest of the book?

No, but why wouldn't you? Answering every single question in the chapter can take less than an hour, and it will prompt so much clarity of intention and creative thought that you'll wonder why you even considered putting it off.

If you're feeling like it's just 'too much trouble', you might be surprised to find that what's stopping you are your own fears about what you're really capable of.

Take a moment now to make a list of any beliefs you are carrying about business or yourself as a business person that might be holding you back.

Here are some typical examples:

It's all too big – I'm only just getting started.
I'm not smart enough to answer these questions.
If I write it down, then I'll have to do it.

Once you've got clear in your own mind what you're saying to stop yourself, simply turn down the volume on those inner voices and begin answering the first question. By the time you've answered at least five questions, the voices in your mind will most likely have quietened themselves, and you'll be well on your way to generating your plan.

CHAPTER ELEVEN

The Three Skills that Lead to Riches

THE THREE SKILLS THAT LEAD TO RICHES

In the late 1980s, I was working as a DJ for Capital Radio in London by day and a stage hypnotist in pubs and clubs by night. While my shows were popular, I couldn't afford to book myself into a proper theatre. I began asking myself some of the wealth-producing questions contained in the 'Simplest Business Plan' chapter, and something jumped out at me – Capital Radio owned one of the most prestigious theatres in London. Was it possible we would be able to do a deal?

After reviewing my options, I decided to make an outrageous request of my boss, Richard Park. I was going to ask him to throw in nearly £200,000 worth of radio advertising with the price of the theatre rental to help me fill the house for the run of the show. I knew that with that added value, the bank would be willing to pick up the majority of the costs in the form of a secured loan.

Despite my preparation, I was convinced he would turn me down. After all, I was asking him to risk not only his money but the reputation of the radio station. When I'd made my pitch, Richard sat back, seemingly deep in thought. Finally, he looked me in the eyes and said three words I'll never forget:

I'll back you!

Ultimately, all success in business comes down to getting other people to say those same three words to you in relation to your business, service or product.

Think about it like this:

Every politician needs people to vote for them. Every shop owner needs people to buy from them. Every actor needs a director to hire them and every filmmaker needs an audience to choose to see their movie at the cinema. In each case, the success or failure of every venture comes down to other people deciding to back you, your service or product.

But people will only back you if you first do three things:

1. **Let them know who you are.**
2. **Tell them the story of what you are offering.**
3. **Convince them it's worth having.**

In this chapter, I will take you through the essence of each of these three skills. Of course, you may be more familiar with them by their 'other' names – networking, marketing and sales.

1. Networking – Letting people know who you are

In the late 1960s, a psychologist called Stanley Milgram decided to run an interesting experiment in the connections between people, also known as 'networks'. One hundred and sixty people in Nebraska were given special packages with instructions to try and get them delivered by hand to a stock-broker who lived in Massachusetts. When Milgram tracked the trail the packages had gone through to reach their target, he found that the average number of steps the package took to get to the stockbroker was between five and six. This is the origin of the phrase 'six degrees of separation'.

The implications of this experiment are profound. Right now, you are no more than six steps away from pretty much anyone on the planet, from a farmer in South Africa to the most famous movie star in the world to the Queen of England. How easy it will be to take those five or six steps is very much dependent on the quality of your network – the people you know and the quality of your relationship with them.

Here's a simple way of thinking about it ...

How many people do you have in your 'fan club'?

While that may seem a strange concept if you are involved in a low-profile pursuit, if you excel at what you do, deliver on what you promise and/or uplift the people around you, you will have one. Your fan club is made up of anyone who admires you and/or what you do and would probably be willing to put in a good word for you if the opportunity arose.

This exercise will help you identify who's currently in your 'fan club' and will focus your mind on where to find more people to join ...

BUILDING YOUR FAN CLUB

1. Create a chart on a piece of paper. Divide the chart into three columns.

2. Head the columns as illustrated below. You can adapt the headings to suit your profession:

Know Who I Am	Experienced my Work	Fan Club

3. Fill in your columns as best you can. You can put in the name of individual people or groups. For example, a friend of mine has a restaurant and is a great chef. She realized that while nearly all the people who'd tasted her cooking had become what management consultant Ken Blanchard calls 'raving fans', not many people had actually heard of her or her restaurant. She worked with her fan club and wealth team to spread the word, and within six months I couldn't even get a table without booking!

4. Brainstorm ideas for helping people move along from one column to the next. For example, if you want more people to experience your work, you may find ways of giving away free samples, or going to a group or organization and offering them a special deal for their members. If you work in an office and want to turn the people who have experienced your work (like your boss and your colleagues) into members of your fan club, you might explore ways of adding more value and doing things above and beyond the call of your job description.

5. Take action on your best ideas. The more action you take, the faster your network will grow and the more members of your fan club you will begin to accumulate.

Remember, it is the members of your fan club who will ultimately be willing to back you as you set out on your road to riches.

2. Marketing – Telling the story of what you have to offer

> *You persuade people with passion, so you've got to have a product or service you feel emotionally charged about. Then you can tell stories about it that will inspire others.*
>
> Dame Anita Roddick, founder of the Body Shop

All of us are involved in communicating every day in some areas of our lives. Marketing is simply the act of communicating the story of your product or service (and remember, if you're an employee that product or service might be *you*) to as many potential buyers as possible with as much energy and focus as you can muster.

What I am suggesting has nothing to do with the kind of bragging and blagging that most of us associate with pushy sales people, but instead is about becoming a *passionate communicator*.

People who are reluctant to communicate to others about their product or service appear not to have a strong belief in the value of what they have to offer. Even if what you are selling is genuinely valuable, it's difficult for other people to buy into it if they don't hear you share the story of it enthusiastically. After all, if someone really believed in their product or service, why would they want to hide it from you?

Of course, before you tell anyone about your product or service, there is someone you need to be absolutely convinced it's worth backing – and that's YOU!

If you aren't passionate about your own product or service, not only will you fail to ignite any interest in other people, you will unconsciously convey to others that you are unsure of its worth, and as a result they will be too.

Stop for a moment and think about your product or service. How passionately do you believe in it on a scale of 1 to 10?

If your answer is below a 10, go to work on your story. You'll find an exercise at the end of this section that will be of great use to you. If your answer is below a 5, you probably need to go back to work on the product or service.

Solving problems before they arise

After you've been telling your story for a while, you'll find that the same concerns come up again and again from your potential clients and customers. Because of this, you can inoculate against these concerns by dealing with them up front, before they even arise.

For example, after years of selling a single weight-loss cassette with great results, the time came to transfer the material to CD. Since I had discovered and developed so many new and powerful techniques for helping people lose weight, I decided to use the transition to expand and update the system.

Instead of just one cassette, my new system would be on five CDs. Instead of just a bit of explanation and a mind-programming technique, my new system would include a number of specific strategies and exercises people could apply immediately to transform their relationship with food, overcome emotional eating, speed up their metabolism, and conquer cravings for ever.

My goal was to create the Rolls Royce of weight-loss programmes, but I knew that some people would be concerned with the higher cost.

When I interrogated my story, I came up with the following analogy:

> *If you join a weight-loss 'club', you will wind up paying over £100 over the course of a year. If you go to see a good therapist who specializes in weight-loss, you'll be paying close to £100 a session, almost certainly over three to five sessions.*
>
> *However, everything that I would do with you if we were doing a personal session together is now available on my new CD system. You pay £48 once – and you can use it as many times as you need. It's like having your own personal weight-loss coach on tap twenty-four hours a day!*

The results speak for themselves. Over the two years we have been selling the new, upgraded CD program, we've sold over 120,000 copies and it's still going strong.

CREATING POWERFUL ANALOGIES

1. Identify the most common problem or objection that people come up with when they hear your story. If you come up with more than one, repeat the exercise with each one in turn.

2. Thinking about the specific problem or objection, complete the following sentence starters at least six times each:

   • This is like …

   • This reminds me of …

   • That would be like …

3. Keep filling in the blanks until you have an analogy that makes you smile, laugh, or simply creates a sense of certainty that what seemed like a problem will not get in the way of the other person getting full value out of your product or service.

Have fun with this – even if you don't use the analogies you come up with, having taken the time to go through this exercise will leave you better prepared and more confident when it comes time to tell your story to someone else.

3. Selling – Asking people to invest in your offering

> *Everyone lives by selling something.*
> ROBERT LOUIS STEVENSON, writer

Like marketing, selling is really just storytelling, but it's about telling a very particular kind of story – a story that engages people's feelings and imagination and motivates them to decide and to act.

Having spent years studying great salespeople, I have distilled the sales process into five simple steps – the same steps that I take each time I want people to back me, my product or service.

Step 1: Know what you want

The key moment in an effective sales conversation usually happens before the conversation even begins. It is the moment you set a clear purpose for the interaction. That purpose can be simple, i.e. 'to connect with them', or more complex, i.e. 'to transmit my fascination with and passion for this product or service'. But to be effective, it must meet these two criteria:

a. It must be based on what you actually want.
   and
b. It must be in terms of what is within your control.

As an example, I once advised a friend of mine who was interviewing for a job with a major investment bank. When I asked him what his goal for the interview was, he said, 'I just don't want to blow it.' Because the mind cannot process a negative, I knew he would be making pictures inside his head of him 'blowing' the interview.

As we've discussed, taking the time to explore the downside is important so that you can take measures to address any potential problems. However, if you spend all your time focused on what might go wrong, you turn it into a self-fulfilling prophecy.

So I said to him, 'No – what do you actually want? What will you see, hear and feel that will let you know the interview went well?' He then described to me the exact look he could imagine seeing in their eyes that would let him know they were impressed with him, and the way they looked at each other and nodded when he answered their questions.

'Now,' I continued, 'what will you do to make that happen? What is your part in creating it?'

He thought for a few moments before responding.

'I just need to prepare like crazy and then be really present in the interview. The rest is up to them.'

Step 2: Find out what *they* really want

Many companies now spend a lot of money on focus groups to find out more about what their customers want, because it gives them the edge on their competitors. But you can get the benefit of a focus group for free every time you speak with a potential customer. Simply ask them what they *really* want and listen carefully to their answers. This will ultimately save you a lot of time, as you can quickly eliminate people from your enquiries if there is no match between what they want and what you've got. It also gives you the information you will need to make amendments to your product or service to better meet the needs and desires of the marketplace.

If you really want to address the concerns of others, one of the best ways is to step into their shoes for a few moments and see the world through their eyes. This was the same process the great Indian leader Gandhi used to convince the occupying British government to leave India and hand control back to the locals without a shot being fired against them.

Gandhi intuitively knew that in order to effectively negotiate the withdrawal, he would need to be able to understand the situation from their point of view. He achieved this in part by a simple process where he would imagine 'stepping in' to the British negotiator, not unlike the way I asked you to step into the great minds of your imaginary advisors in chapter eight. When looking at the situation from the British perspective, he could see what was most important to them and was able to formulate a plan that allowed all sides to perceive great value in the agreement.

SEEING THROUGH THE EYES OF YOUR CUSTOMERS

1. Imagine 'stepping in' to several of your customers and seeing things from their perspective.

2. From inside your customer's mind, ask yourself:

   What do I want?

   What are my biggest concerns?

   What do I need to see and hear to feel good about this?

   What would be best for everyone?

3. Incorporate your insights into your story – when you can imagine loving your proposition through their eyes, you're on your way to success!

Step 3: Interrogate your story

Mark Burnett is the most successful TV producer in the world and has made hundreds of millions of pounds from his genius ideas and productions, changing the face of television with shows like *Survivor* and *The Apprentice*. When I first approached him about our doing a show together, he spent four hours interrogating me about every aspect of the show – who it was for, how it worked, what could go wrong and how we could fix it. He also did something very important – he showed me how to turn every single feature of the show into a benefit.

For example, one of the features I was most proud of was that we would be able to do personal change work directly through the television with the viewer sitting at home. Mark pointed out that, to the end user, what mattered wasn't that we would be doing personal change work but that they would be able to lose weight, quit smoking and feel better about themselves and their lives. All too often people enthuse about the technical specs of their product when all the end user cares about is what it will do for them.

The simple rule of thumb is this:

Always focus on the benefits!

At the end of our time together, I not only knew all the benefits of the show to the network and viewing audience, I also knew every potential problem we might face and how to solve it. Although there were only a few concerns raised in the meetings by the network executives, we were able to quickly allay their fears because we had anticipated them.

Better still, by the end of Mark's 'interrogation', I was absolutely convinced that what were going to pitch was fantastic. I knew in every fibre of my being that we had a brilliant show, one that I could talk about with passion.

Do this exercise for yourself now ...

INTERROGATING YOUR STORY

1. Stop for a moment and write down all the positive value that your product or service will bring to your customers. Remember to focus on benefits, not features. You need to tell yourself these benefits over and over again before you tell your story to anybody else.

2. Next, I'd like you to deliberately think about a negative – any reason why people might not want to back your product or service and find the solution. Be sure to write these down – if you try to do this step in your head you will tend to overwhelm yourself!

3. Now, for each item on your list, come up with a solution – either a way of solving the problem, mitigating the problem or, better still, eliminating it as a problem altogether.

4. Tell your story with passion to at least five people who *aren't* potential customers each day for a week. This is so you won't feel like you are 'selling', and will be able to put your full attention on refining the quality of your story.

Remember, the meaning of your communication is the response you get, so if your story isn't exciting to you and your listeners, change it!

Step 4: Get yourself into a great state

There are essentially three things you need to do to put yourself into an optimal state for selling:

a. Make rich pictures in your mind of yourself succeeding.
b. Speak to yourself in a confident, positive tone of voice.
c. Move your body decisively, with a sense of comfort and ease.

You can shortcut the process by using your 'rich' anchor, which you created at the very beginning of this book. Simply put your thumb and middle finger together and feel the feelings of being rich – living life on your own terms and following your possibilities.

The reason the rich state is also the optimal selling state is simple – when you are already feeling rich, you do not need to make the sale. And in sales, nothing puts people off more than the 'smell' of a desperate salesperson!

Step 5: Tell your story and ask for what you want

In the end, sales is a numbers game. While you can improve your percentages with additional practice and additional techniques, the basic maths will always hold:

The more people you talk to, the more people will buy whatever it is you are selling.

Ultimately there is only one way to get others to back you and that is to tell them what you want and ask them to do it. Some people are scared to do this in case they get rejected. But rich thinkers think about it differently. They know that when you ask for what you want, you will always get one of three answers:

- Yes
- No
- Maybe

They believe in the value of their product and they know that the money, backing and resources they need are out there. So if somebody decides not to buy from them or to back them, it's either because a) the person doesn't yet understand the benefits to them or b) it really isn't what they want or need in that moment.

In this sense, the sooner you can eliminate the people who don't want or need what you've got from your enquiries, the sooner you can connect the right people with what you have on offer.

If you ever find yourself worrying about telling your story or reluctant to ask a potential customer for a sale, change the game for good by using this exercise adapted from my book *Instant Confidence* ...

FINDING YOUR IDEAL CLIENTS AND CUSTOMERS

Read through this exercise before you do it for the first time …

1. Make a list of exactly twenty names of people or companies who might want what you have.

2. The objective of the game is to get rid of anyone on the list who does NOT want to back you or buy from you. Get in touch with each person on the list and get a 'yes' or 'no' as quickly as possible – don't take 'maybe' for an answer!

3. Give yourself a score at the end of the day, based on the number of names left on your list. The goal is to get your score below ten each day – in other words, eliminate at least ten people from your enquiries each and every day. If you 'accidentally' find someone who DOES want to back you or buy from you, you can take them off the list as well.

Keep track of your scores – if you can get down to zero five working days in a row, you will have transformed your business and jumpstarted your accumulation of wealth.

FREQUENTLY ASKED QUESTIONS ABOUT 'THE THREE SKILLS THAT LEAD TO RICHES':

Q. I'm not a natural networker and I'm certainly not a salesperson. Do I really have to learn these skills to make money?

A lot of people in Britain have an image of a salesperson as a slick-haired, slick-talking con artist. While there are certainly people who work in sales who fit that description, the best salespeople are the ones who never feel like they're selling. They're more 'spokespeople' – advocates for their product or service who are excited about telling their story.

You don't have to be a 'natural' to succeed – just talk to people and tell your story, and before you know it you'll have developed the skills that will serve you in every area of your life.

Remember, it's not about persuasion, it's about passionate presentation. Talk about your passion and people will connect with you and resonate. If they don't buy, it will be because it genuinely isn't the right fit for them in this moment, not because you didn't 'sell them' hard enough.

Of course, if you can't muster any passion for your product or service, you're either in the wrong business or telling the wrong story!

Q. I'm applying for jobs at the moment so, in a way, I'm my own product. Can I use the 'three skills' to sell myself?

Absolutely! Whether you're selling a photocopier, bag of peanuts, cleaning service or yourself as a job applicant, you're essentially selling a service and/or a product. When you think about it that way, you can dissociate from the 'but it's me' phenomenon and look at yourself objectively.

Use your network to get referrals, insights and recommendations; interrogate your story to get the word out in a way that your target market will want to hear it, and use the five-step sales process to put your best foot forward in every interview.

Will you get the job every time? No – and you wouldn't want to. You want the best fit for you and your skills, not 'any job at any cost'. When you approach the process in this way, you will find yourself quickly screening possible users of your services so you wind up with the perfect employers for your unique talents and skills.

Q. Am I supposed to go through all the exercises in the sales process every time I sell something? It seems a little bit complex to me!

The idea behind the five-step process is to give yourself the optimal preparation – once you've gone through it, forget about it and focus on the person you have in front of you. Speak naturally, prep your unconscious, trust your unconscious, then go for it. You may be surprised at how much of what you prepared will 'naturally' tumble out of you when you are in front of your potential customer.

CHAPTER TWELVE

The Secrets of Living Rich

THE SECRETS OF LIVING RICH

> *For the past 33 years, I have looked in the mirror every morning and asked myself: If today were the last day of my life, would I want to do what I am about to do today?*
> *And whenever the answer has been no for too many days in a row, I know I need to change something.*
>
> STEVE JOBS,
> billionaire founder
> of Apple Computers

In a fascinating study done at the University of London, a team of researchers developed a happiness scale, designed to measure people's relative sense of wellbeing from moment to moment. They then devised a formula to calculate how much extra money the average person would have to earn every year to get the same level of happiness as they would from the simple pleasures of a rich life.

For instance, having an active social life brought the equivalent satisfaction of a £63,844 annual salary increase, while living with a loved one was found to bring the same amount of satisfaction as being given an £82,500 annual pay rise. Good health was found to be the most valuable aspect of wellbeing – having a 'clean bill of health' was equated to a £304,000-a-year pay rise!

Yet, for all this, money still can't buy happiness. As a society we are better paid, fed, educated and housed than ever before in history, yet since the 1950s we have become less and less happy. Statistics show there has never been so much depression in the world as there is right now.

The reasons for this may surprise you ...

Wealth dysmorphia

Over the years I have worked with many people who have body dysmorphia, a condition where someone distorts their view of themselves to such a degree that they cannot bear to look in the mirror because they believe themselves to be hideously ugly.

This has nothing to do with how someone really looks – it is an internal filter that searches for everything that is wrong and blocks out everything that is right. So someone with this condition will focus upon some tiny aspect of their appearance that they don't like – say a wrinkle or a fold of skin – to the exclusion of everything else.

What's interesting is how many people do the same thing with money – they filter out all the areas of their life where they are already rich and focus on what's missing from their lives instead.

An exercise I often do with my clients is to ask them to imagine that, for whatever reason, money is no longer an issue in their lives. Within the realms of physical reality, they are free to pursue whatever they want to be, do or have.

I then ask them to make two lists. The first list is of all the things they would change; the second is of everything they can think of that would stay the same. What is remarkable is how little most people would actually change their lives if they had more money.

Sure, they might switch jobs, take more holidays, get a nicer car or move to a larger house – but they wouldn't dump their friends, stop visiting their favourite restaurants, watch different movies or laugh at different things.

Here's the payoff:

Everything you wouldn't change if you had more money is an area of your life where you are already living rich!

True and lasting happiness never is and never will be the result of how much money you have in the bank – it's the product of living a life rich in value, meaning and purpose. That's why being happy and living rich are experiences you can begin to cultivate now, regardless of how much or how little money you are already making.

The more you focus on those areas where you are already rich, the more you will realize how wealthy you already are.

I began this book by suggesting that you are already rich in ways that you do not realize. Now, I will go a step further:

There are many ways in which you are already as rich as the wealthiest billionaire on the planet.

For example:

- Any time you have a good night's sleep, you are 'sleeping rich'. A billionaire may be able to buy a more expensive mattress, but they can't buy themselves a more restful night.
- Any time you go into a restaurant and can order anything on the menu, you are having the exact same experience of possibility and abundance as the wealthiest man or woman alive.
- Any time you walk down a beach or look up at a sunset, you are experiencing the same beauty and splendour as the most financially well-off person in the world.

In their book *The Maui Millionaire*, authors Diane Kennedy and David Finkel make this point in a very direct and somewhat shocking way:

Some people think that everything has its price. Well, if that's true, how much would it take for you to sell your ability to see? Would you accept a million dollars in return for your ability to see? How about ten million dollars?

What about your ability to move? How much would you sell your ability to walk for? How about your ability to move your arms? Would you trade them for any amount of money?

What about your past? What would you sell all your memories for? Would you trade all your memories, good and bad, leaving you bereft of any past, for a million dollars?

*What about the love of your friends and family? What would
your price be to trade for these precious relationships?*

*Just take a moment to reflect on the people, things, abilities,
and experiences you are most grateful for in your life.*

*Now, how wealthy are you really? On a scale from one to ten,
how wealthy are you when you stop and look at the full picture
of your life?*

While this can be an uncomfortable exercise for some people,
the point is clear – what we take for granted in our lives is
invariably priceless. In this sense, the reason so many people
feel poor is because they are already so rich. They have
stopped paying attention to all the good that is a constant in
their lives, and are only noticing the situations where unex-
pected problems break through into their consciousness.

So why don't we usually appreciate what we already
have?

Surprisingly, the problem isn't with our values, or even
with our society – it's with the hardwiring of our brains.

The process of habituation

Our brains are designed to 'habituate' repeated experience. What that means is that once any behaviour or experience has been repeated a certain number of times, our conscious mind will stop paying attention to it. This is an efficient system in some respects, because it allows the limited attention of the conscious mind to be available for spotting difference, which is a harbinger of danger. Where it works against us is that when much of our daily life is made up of the same types of stimuli, our lives can appear mundane no matter how wonderful they actually are.

The good news is that this 'trick of the mind' is not one we are stuck with. In contrast, everything we have done in this book so far has been designed to reset your patterns of habituation so you can live a richer and richer life.

In one study of habituation, three Zen masters were placed in a room with their eyes closed and a clicking sound was made twenty times in a row at precise fifteen-second intervals. When this study had been attempted with 'ordinary' people, the monitoring of their brainwave patterns revealed that by the fifth click, habituation had set in and the control subjects no longer noticed the clicking noise.

In sharp contrast, the Zen masters responded to each repeated stimulus as fully as they had to the first. It was as if their openness to the experience of each moment resulted in their perceiving the world anew in each moment.

That openness to the moment is one that can be cultivated, simply by taking time each day to interrupt the sense of sameness that can deaden our senses to the fullness and possibility of the 'now'. We can reset the equilibrium and begin once again to notice the richness of our lives.

Here's an exercise that will help you to interrupt your patterns by changing the habitual questions you ask yourself. Be sure to take the time not only to ask these questions, but also to answer them.

WEALTH-REVEALING QUESTIONS

1. Who or what in my life makes me feel happiest?

2. Who or what in my life brings me the greatest pleasure?

3. Who or what in my life makes me feel most loved?

4. What is it in my life that brings me the greatest feeling of satisfaction?

5. What is it in my life that makes it feel meaningful?

6. Who or what am I most grateful for in my life?

7. Who or what in my life makes me feel richest?

If you ask and answer these questions at least three times a day for the next three weeks, you will be amazed at the transformation you will experience in your life!

The Pareto Principle

The 19th-century economist Wilfred Pareto was the first to discover that approximately 80 per cent of the world's wealth was concentrated in the hands of only 20 per cent of the world's population. While this was startling in and of itself, what was even more remarkable to him was that this '80/20' rule seemed to hold true in nearly every area of our lives.

Although the numbers are rarely this exact, here are some of the ways statisticians have recorded the impact of the 'Pareto Principle' in our society today:

- 80 per cent of the loss value of all crimes comes from 20 per cent of the criminals.
- 80 per cent of all car accidents are caused by 20 per cent of the motorists.
- 80 per cent of divorces involve only 20 per cent of married people (many people divorce multiple times).

In the 1960s, IBM 're-discovered' the Pareto Principle when they realized that 80 per cent of their computers' operating time was spent executing 20 per cent of their programming. By focusing their efforts exclusively on that 20 per cent, they were able to create massive upgrades in the effectiveness and usability of their computers in a remarkably short period of time. Today, many of the world's leading corporations are using this principle to increase efficiencies, maximize profits and produce more with less.

Check to see how many of these 80/20 patterns are present in your own life:

- 80 per cent of your results come from 20 per cent of your efforts.
- 80 per cent of your job satisfaction comes from 20 per cent of your work.
- 80 per cent of the wear on your carpets takes place on 20 per cent of the area.
- 80 per cent of the time you wear 20 per cent of your clothes.
- 80 per cent of your rich feelings come from 20 per cent of your experiences.

What is so amazing about this principle is that once you begin noticing it, you will see it everywhere. And once you begin acting on it, you will be able to sort for where the money-making and happiness opportunities are in your life with an almost scientific precision.

In my own life, this simple idea has had a most profound impact. I first used it to analyse my business and discovered that approximately 80 per cent of my profits came from 20 per cent of my projects. Over the next six months, I redoubled my efforts on that all-important 20 per cent and increased my profits by nearly 2,000 per cent over the course of that year.

Next, I looked at those areas of the business I particularly enjoyed and those I didn't. Sure enough, about 80 per cent of my stress was coming from 20 per cent of my customers. I began phasing out my work with those customers immediately. Once again, the return in energy and happiness was dramatic.

Finally, I began to apply the Pareto Principle in my personal life. By continually focusing on the 20 per cent of activities and friends that brought me 80 per cent of my pleasure, satisfaction and meaning, I was able to experience far more happiness in far less time than ever before.

While the numbers will not always work out in these exact proportions, the thing to realize is that not all opportunities are equally valuable and not all activities are equally worthwhile. By removing high-effort/low-reward activities and people from your life and focusing your energy instead on those things that require less effort but bring in a far greater reward, you can continually refocus your priorities with a laser-like intensity.

You will find yourself moving forward with less effort and more income, less busy work and more time, and perhaps best of all less stress and more freedom than ever before.

DOING MORE WITH LESS

1. Do an '80/20 audit' on each of the most important areas of your life. Ask yourself these questions now:

   • What are the 20 per cent of your customers and work efforts that are leading to 80 per cent of your profits?

   • What are the 20 per cent of your customers and work efforts that give you 80 per cent of your problems?

   • What are the 20 per cent of activities and areas of your life in which you experience 80 per cent of your happiness?

2. Based on what you've learned, what should you be doing less of? What would be worth doing more of?

3. What are the one, two or three activities you engage in which create results out of all proportion to the amount of time and energy you invest in them?

4. If you only had one month to live, how would you spend your time? How many of those activities can you bring into your life this week?

5. Ask yourself Steve Jobs's question:

   **If today were the last day of my life,
   would I want to do what I am about to do today?**

The more you can answer 'yes' to this question, the richer your life will become!

As you complete this exercise and begin to experience its implications in your own life, you will realize that doing more with less is one of the absolute keys to living rich, as it gives you the luxury of more energy and the luxury of more time to apply that energy to doing those things that truly bring you joy.

And figuring out how to spend your money and how to spend your time can be one of the most rewarding activities of all.

The joy of living rich

> *Anyone who thinks money will make you happy hasn't got money. Happy is harder than money.*
>
> DAVID GEFFEN, billionaire film producer

Having worked as a therapist for over twenty years, I am continually struck by the general lack of joy in people's lives. Some people experience hardly any good feelings during the course of a day. Because that's what they are used to, they think it's natural. What I point out to them is that a lack of joy in life isn't natural – it's normal. But 'normal' is just another way of saying 'what usually happens'. In parts of the world, poverty is 'normal'. Children dying of hunger is 'normal'. Cruelty to animals is 'normal'.

The point is, 'normal' doesn't mean good, and it certainly doesn't mean 'natural'. Natural is what you're designed for – and, simply put, human beings are designed for happiness.

Because feeling rich, joyful and happy are neurophysiological states, they operate according to our basic principle from chapter one:

What you focus on, you get more of.

Your mind learns through the process of generalization. As a child, you learned how a door opens; you then generalized that information and instantly understood how most doors open. If it wasn't for your ability to generalize, you would spend time each day relearning how to go in and out of a room.

Happiness works the same way. Like any other emotional state, the more you think about abundance, wellbeing and joy, the more you get to feel them. Better still, you can amplify each one of these feelings and make them much more intense than you 'normally' experience them.

In our final exercise together, we're going to increase your daily levels of joy. We're going to transform the 'background stress' so many people live with day after day into 'background happiness'. You will automatically experience more and more states of rich, joyful happiness more of the time and throughout the day.

As we crank up your 'happiness thermostat', you will still be able to feel a full dynamic range of emotions, but the base line, the default settings of your happiness, will be much higher. You will have this overwhelming feeling that everything is really working out for the best – you are already rich in so many ways. You can then use the hypnosis CD to 'lock in' these changes for good.

In order to get maximum value from this exercise, you may want to first review the list of your highest values you created in chapter six …

CREATING A RICH FUTURE

Read through this exercise in its entirety before you begin.

1. Squeeze your thumb and middle finger together on each hand and fire off your rich anchor. When you have at least a taste of your richest feelings, let the anchor go for now.

2. One by one, go through each of your highest values. Vividly imagine experiencing each one. If it's 'love', remember times you have felt deeply loving and truly loved. If it's 'freedom', remember or imagine experiences of being incredibly alive and free.

3. As you imagine experiencing each value in turn, add them in to your rich anchor. Squeeze your thumb and finger together on both hands and reinforce the link between the good feelings of your values and the squeeze of your thumb and fingers.

4. Repeat steps 2 and 3 until you are almost overwhelmed by good feelings. Allow yourself to feel even more wonderful than you are used to doing.

5. Now, as you continue to hold your rich anchor, imagine taking these good feelings into all of the major areas of your life – home, family, career, community and the world at large. Imagine feeling this good even in difficult situations, and how much better things will turn out when you go into them feeling this way.

6. Imagine what it would be like to wake up each day, feeling this good. What would it be like tomorrow? Next week? Next month? Next year? Five years from now? Ten years from now?

7. Look at your timeline and make sure it's filled with pictures of you looking healthy, happy and truly rich now and on into the future. Make sure that you are always in the pictures, looking good and feeling great.

8. Finally, float into the most appealing pictures on your time-line and vividly imagine what it will be like to live your values while adding value to the world, doing good and feeling amazing!

Each time you do this exercise, you are not only flooding your body with good feelings, you are increasing your capacity for joy. And when you think joyfully about your future, you are programming your mind for a lifetime of happiness and riches beyond measure.

FREQUENTLY ASKED QUESTIONS ABOUT 'THE SECRETS OF LIVING RICH'

Q. I'm terrified that if I really allow myself to feel rich before I have a lot of money, I'll wind up not doing what it takes to actually make the money. What do you suggest?

Before you do anything else, review the material in chapter five and tap away the fear. Nothing clouds our ability to think clearly and make good decisions like fear, anger or greed.

Then, when you're feeling better in yourself, review your rich vision. If you've created goals for yourself that really inspire you, they'll pull you forward and keep you in action without the constant threat of fear of poverty nipping at your heels. If not, go back and create goals that will!

Q. I've realized that 80 per cent of my stress in life comes from 1 per cent of the people –my partner! Do I need to leave them in order to live rich?

There are very few people I know who would say their life has been enriched by divorce or the break-up of a long-term romantic relationship. In fact, most of the rich thinkers I studied for this book have been with the same partner for most of their adult lives.

Obviously, if you are in an emotionally or physically abusive relationship, it is important to seek outside help. But before you go running off into the sunset with someone else, take the time to explore these other 80/20 questions:

- What are the 20 per cent of the issues that cause 80 per cent of our arguments? How could we most easily resolve them?
- What are the 20 per cent of the shared activities that lead to 80 per cent of our positive experiences? How can we make the time to do even more of them?

As you explore your relationship in this way, you may find that you are able to transform even the most difficult of relationships and reconnect with the love that originally brought you together.

Q. Why is it always the people with money who say 'the best things in life are free'?

It's because the people who already have money *know* that money really can't buy happiness, whereas people who don't yet have much money still believe that it can.

Part of my purpose in writing this book is to give you a chance to find that out for yourself. In the end, I will be delighted if you write to tell me how much money you have made as a result of using this system, but I will be even more delighted when you share how much richer your life has become!

A FINAL NOTE FROM PAUL

A few years ago, the renowned scientist and researcher Rupert Sheldrake came to my house to conduct a series of experiments into the power of human thoughts to influence the thoughts and feelings of others. Sceptical as I was when we began, the results of the experiments were so conclusively positive that I had to begin opening my mind to new possibilities.

I then came across some research into the effects of focused intention on an even more dramatic scale. In 1993, a group of 4,000 experienced meditators came together in Washington DC for a period of three weeks. All 4,000 people spent an hour twice a day focused on sending peaceful thoughts out into the city. The results, while controversial, were astounding. The rate of violent crime in the city fell by over 20 per cent.

It seems that our collective thoughts really do have an impact upon our physical reality. As Gandhi said, 'You must be the change you want to see in the world.'

May your search for the riches within you make the world around you a richer place!

God bless you

Paul McKenna

INDEX OF EXERCISES

---- TO TRAIN PERSONALLY WITH ----
PAUL McKENNA

call 0845 230 2022
www.paulmckenna.com